THE
Long-Term
Day Trader

100101010010111
10111010101101
1010001110101
1010101001000
1111010101010
1010101010110
10101011010010
1011101010010
100101010010111
100010101001100
1010001110101
1010101001000
1111010101010
1010101010110
10101011010010
10111010101101
11010101101
1010001110101
1010101001000
1111010101010
1010101010110
10101011010010
10111010101101
100010101001100
1010001110101
1010101001000
1111010101010
1010101010110
10101011010010
10111010101101
100010101001100
1010001110101
1010101001000
1111010101010
1010101010110
10101011010010
10111010101101
100010101001100
1010001110101
1010101001000
1111010101010
1010101010110
10101011010010
1011101010010

THE
Long-Term
Day Trader

Short-Term Strategies
to Boost Your
Long-Term Profits

Michael Sincere
& Deron Wagner

CAREER
PRESS

Franklin Lakes, NJ

THE LONG-TERM DAY TRADER
Cover design by Design Solutions
Printed in the U.S.A. by Book-mart Press

To order this title, please call toll-free 1-800-CAREER-1 (NJ and Canada: 201-848-0310) to order using VISA or MasterCard, or for further information on books from Career Press.

CAREER
PRESS

The Career Press, Inc., 3 Tice Road, PO Box 687, Franklin Lakes, NJ 07417
www.careerpress.com

Library of Congress Cataloging-in-Publication Data

Sincere, Michael.
    The long-term day trader : short-term strategies to boost your long-term
profits / by Michael Sincere and Deron Wagner.
        p.   cm.
    Includes index.
    ISBN 1-56414-453-4 (paper)
    1. Day trading (Securities) 2. Securities. 3. Securities industry. 4. Investment
analysis. I. Wagner, Deron. II. Title.

HG4515.95 .S53 2000
332.64′2′0285—dc21   00-024908

Dedication

This book is dedicated to Gwenola and Rachele.

Acknowledgments

It usually takes a group of dedicated people working together to complete a non-fiction book. With this in mind, we would like to recognize Mark Cook, Barry Dorfman, David Nassar, Linda Raschke, and Oliver Velez, who accepted our invitations to be interviewed and who shared their day-trading strategies. We'd also like to thank Halbert Uy, a short-term after-hours trader and manager of a hedge fund, Proteus Capital Partners, L.P., for providing valuable editorial and technical assistance. We thank our publisher, Ron Fry, for his continued support with all our projects, Stacey Farkas and Karen Prager for their editing guidance, Michael Gaffney and Jackie Michaels from Career Press for their promotional efforts, and Internet developer Magnus Bergsson for designing our interactive Web site. We are in awe of how everything always seems to work out for the best.

—The Authors

◀ ◀ ▶ ▶

I would like to thank Joanne Pessin for her phenomenal organizational skills. Without her help, this book would never have been finished on time. I am also grateful to Andy Whelchel and Jason Cangialosi, my agents, who listened to all my book ideas and encouraged me to keep writing. I appreciate the work of Alecia Berman, my meticulous and hard-working researcher, who uncovered more about day trading than I thought possible. I also thank those who continue to believe in my work: Alexandra Bengtsson, Angela Bengtsson, Johanna Segeman, Anna Frankenberg, Nina Carlsson, Line Kristensen, Magali Ringoot, Gunda Gramkow, Isabelle Giroux, Lauren Lispi, Jenny Rydholm, Tine Claes,

Miriam and Brian Vanstraten, John and Carolyn Bredesen, Anna Ridolfo, Lois Sincere, and Charles Sincere. Finally, I'd like to thank the staff at Starbucks in Mizner Park for serving great coffee and providing a superb writing environment.

—Michael Sincere

I would like to thank Terry Townsend, who helped get my trading career started; Rose Kessler, for all her hard work in transcribing the tapes; and Barry Dorfman, for his knowledge and inspiration. I also want to thank the staff of Investor's Street for their support, Kerry Stanley for his editing efforts, and Richard Wagner for reviewing my material. Finally, my thanks to my wife, Rachele, for her help on this project, and to Mark Cole, John Lakatis, Mark Fahnestock, Ed Balog, Mike Reiter, Michael Paules, and Mike Bradford.

—Deron Wagner

Contents

Long-Term Day Trading

I t took awhile before I actually believed that you could make money as a short-term trader. After all, I grew up in a family of stockbrokers who instilled in me an almost religious belief in the importance of a long-term buy-and-hold strategy. While acquaintances of mine were flitting in and out of the market with various degrees of success, I watched the value of my investments, especially my mutual funds, multiply and grow. It seemed so easy it was almost embarrassing.

And yet I'd often meet extremely successful short-term traders who made my long-term returns look like a joke. I saw evidence of 150 percent returns, 200 percent returns. A 33-year-old California woman named Wendy Miele gave up practicing law for trading and in one year turned $5,000 into $250,000. Like many people, I believed the media reports that characterized day traders as bleary-eyed, burned-out zombies who could blow up at any minute. Actually, I discovered that most are honest, hard-working people quietly making a living at something they truly love.

After months of research, including a week of training in day trading, I've concluded that there is a lot of confusion about the true meaning of day trading. As far as many people on Wall Street are concerned, anyone who doesn't use a stockbroker is a day trader. Many financial reporters fail to correct this misconception, mistakenly identifying all short-term traders as day traders, regardless of their strategies.

As it turns out, I've learned there are as many day-trading strategies as investment strategies. Although we will discuss these in more detail, the most difficult day-trading strategy is intra-day trading, a strategy that involves buying and selling dozens of stocks within a few minutes or hours, sometimes just to make small 1/16 or 1/8 profits. When the media talk about day trading, this is usually the strategy they are referring to.

A large number of day traders, however, use a combination of short-term strategies, from intra-day trading to swing trading—holding a stock for one to five days but aiming for much larger profits. For example, Wendy Miele, the woman with the 1,000 percent yearly returns, usually makes no more than one trade a day but holds her stocks for several days. She uses both intra-day and swing trading strategies.

Another example is my co-author, Deron Wagner, an experienced short-term trader who uses a variety of day-trading strategies to make money in the market. He makes only a few trades a day but watches them closely. He spends more time analyzing stocks than trading, which could be one of the secrets of his success. He picks only the trading opportunities that have the best chance for success and ignores everything else. What is most exciting about Deron's tactics is that his strategies work in both bull and bear markets. When the inevitable bear market comes, and it will one day, panicked investors will sell to lock in their profits. That's when many short-term traders will really clean up.

You might think the title of our book is an oxymoron. After all, how can someone be a long-term investor and day trade? It is actually quite simple. A portion of my portfolio is comfortably invested in high-quality stocks, mutual funds, and index funds. At the same time, I use a small part of my portfolio to aggressively buy and sell stocks using the short-term strategies included in this book.

Will you make money using the strategies of a short-term trader? There is no way to predict who will be successful, but I do know this: After reading our book, you will never invest the same way again. After all, why should you be limited to only one investment strategy? Proponents of both schools claim to have the key to wealth, and the truth is, they are both correct. You can make a fortune buying and holding stocks for a lifetime, but you can also make money on a short-term basis. When you combine the time-tested strategies of a classic buy-and-hold investor with those of a short-term trader, you end up being what we call *long-term day traders*. It took months of research, analysis, and conversations with other traders for us to create this strategy.

In our book, we will show you how to use short-term strategies, with an emphasis on technical analysis, to boost your profits in the market. Because this book is written by a traditional buy-and-hold investor and a practicing day trader, you will get the benefit of both perspectives.

Although we geared this book to long-term investors who have never tried their hand at short-term trading, we also believe that novice day traders might pick up a few tips and ideas. We think the book will be especially useful to those who have been unsuccessful with intra-day trading strategies such as "trading the teenies" and "scalping." These strategies are much harder to master than most people think. As you might know, as many as 90 to 95 percent of intra-day traders fail to make a profit after one year of trading. We hope that some of the strategies and tactics introduced here will help to improve the success rates of beginning day traders.

In the first section of the book, we give you an overview of how to get started as a long-term day trader. We describe the computer equipment you need and the reasons to consider using a combination of investment strategies. We want to show you that anyone can use long-term day trading to make substantial profits in the market.

In the next section, we describe the short-term strategies you can use to boost your investment returns. As you might guess, there is a heavy emphasis on technical analysis, but we make it as user-friendly as possible, with charts to help explain some of the more difficult concepts.

We also teach you how to make money no matter how the market is doing. Even if we enter a bear market or there is a huge correction, short-term traders can profit. In fact, many professional short-term traders make more money during a bear market than a bull market. We will teach you how to profit from, rather than fear, a market correction.

Although the technical rules are extremely important, we don't forget about another important area: trading psychology. No matter how you buy or sell stocks, either as a short-term trader or a long-term investor, the way you handle your emotions will determine how successful you will be. In fact, most pros admit that mastering emotions is the hardest part of their job. Whether you realize it or not, psychology plays a part with every trade you make, especially when you are trading with your own money.

While doing research for this book, I made an interesting discovery: The most profitable long-term investors and short-term traders share many of the same personality traits. Both are disciplined and passionate about their work, think fast under pressure, and trade stocks without getting emotional. The difference is that day traders depend on a variety of short-term technical data to determine which stocks to buy and sell, while long-term investors depend primarily on fundamental data. Just like the best investors, the best traders lose less money and make fewer mistakes than other traders.

The second section also includes tips on the most effective way to manage your trades, including what many pros consider the key to profits: discipline. While other traders eventually succumb to fear or greed, the two most common emotions, the pros stick to their strategies without exception. The top traders seem to have an amazing amount of discipline. If everyone were so disciplined, a lot more people would be making a lot more money in the market.

Perhaps what I enjoyed the most in writing this book was conducting interviews with the best of the best short-term traders. To be a successful short-term trader, you must find out what works for other traders. Each of the short-term traders I interviewed uses one or more day-trading strategies. For example, I talked with Barry Dorfman, a successful swing trader and president of Trader's Choice, a consulting and marketing company for Wall Street trading firms. Barry reveals many of the secrets of his success and tells you exactly what you need to do to be a profitable short-term trader.

Then you will meet Oliver Velez, president and co-founder of Pristine.com, a firm for self-directed traders, and co-author of *Advanced Tools and Tactics for the Master Day Trader* (McGraw-Hill). Oliver has had an extremely successful 11-year track record in the day-trading industry as a trainer and trader.

I also talked extensively with Mark Cook, considered by many to be one of the best intra-day traders in the country. He reveals how he's consistently made money scalping stocks for more than 20 years, defying the statistics and confounding nearly all of his critics.

You will also meet Linda Bradford Raschke, a consistently profitable day trader first profiled in Jack Schwager's best-selling *New Market Wizards* (HarperBusiness) and in Sue Herera's *Women of the Street* (John Wiley and Sons). Linda is recognized as one of the top traders in the country.

Finally, I interviewed David Nassar, president and CEO of Market Wise Securities and author of the best-selling *How to Get Started in Electronic Day Trading* (McGraw-Hill), the book that revolutionized the day-trading industry and turned thousands of online investors into day traders. David explains the importance of trading psychology and discusses a few of the methods he uses to minimize risk.

Deron and I have enjoyed sharing our knowledge with you. Our ultimate goal was to write an entertaining, informative book about short-term trading that will teach you how to make money no matter what the market is doing. It's not always easy to be entertaining when you are writing about support and resistance levels, trend reversals, and sector trading, but we did our best.

Our intent is not to turn you into a professional day trader. Rather, we hope to show you that some of the most aggressive short-term tactics can improve your overall investment returns. The idea is to help you make as much money as possible in the shortest amount of time—and still get a good night's sleep. If we can do that, then we have achieved our goal.

No matter what you think about our book, never stop trying to improve your short-term trading skills. If you are passionate about trading, if you are disciplined about following the rules in this book, and if you are willing to learn how to be a better trader, nothing should stop you from generating wealth for yourself and your family. It's not easy, but if you work hard and apply what you've learned here, we believe you can be successful. Some of the best opportunities to make money in the stock market are yet to come. With a little luck and a lot of work, this could be your most profitable year yet. We wish you all the best.

—Michael Sincere

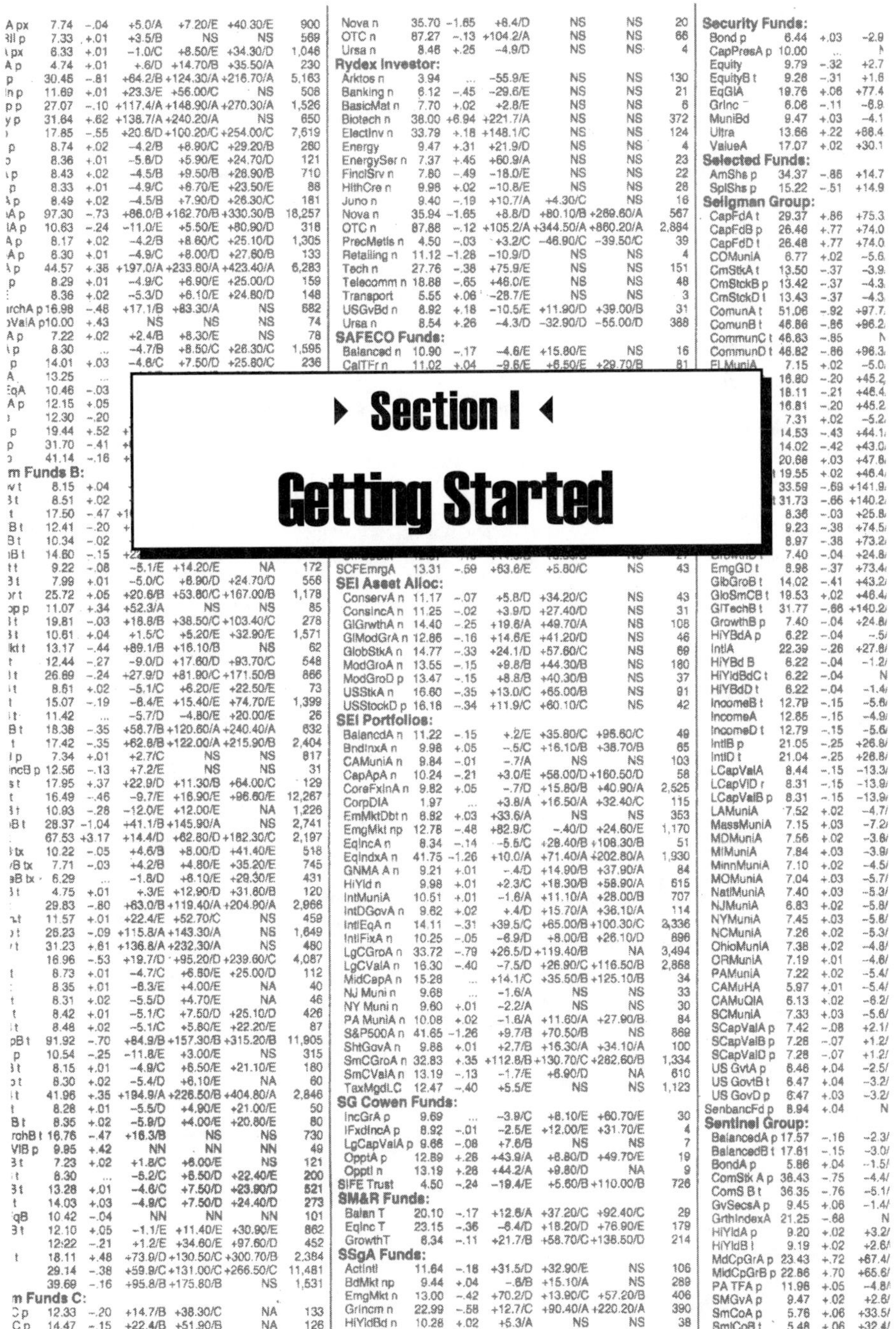

▶ Section I ◀
Getting Started

A px	7.74	-.04	+5.0/A	+7.20/E	+40.30/E	900	Nova n	35.70	-1.65	+8.4/D	NS	NS	20	**Security Funds:**
Rll p	7.33	+.01	+3.5/B	NS	NS	569	OTC n	87.27	-.13	+104.2/A	NS	NS	66	Bond p	6.44	+.03	-2.9
Lpx	6.33	+.01	-1.0/C	+8.50/E	+34.30/D	1,048	Ursa n	8.46	+.25	-4.9/D	NS	NS	4	CapPresA p	10.00	...	N
A p	4.74	+.01	+.6/D	+14.70/B	+35.50/A	230	**Rydex Investor:**							Equity	9.79	-.32	+2.7
p	30.45	-.81	+64.2/B	+124.30/A	+216.70/A	5,163	Arktos n	3.94	...	-55.9/E	NS	NS	130	EquityBt	9.28	-.11	+1.6
In p	11.69	+.01	+23.3/E	+56.00/C	NS	508	Banking n	6.12	-.45	-29.6/E	NS	NS	21	EqGIA	19.76	+.06	+77.4
p p	27.07	-.10	+117.4/A	+148.90/A	+270.30/A	1,526	BasicMat n	7.70	+.02	+2.8/E	NS	NS	6	GrInc t	6.06	-.11	-5.9
y p	31.64	+.62	+138.7/A	+240.20/A	NS	650	Biotech n	38.00	+8.94	+221.7/A	NS	NS	372	MuniBd	9.47	+.03	-4.1
)	17.85	-.55	+20.6/D	+100.20/C	+254.00/C	7,519	ElectInv n	33.79	+.18	+148.1/C	NS	NS	124	Ultra	13.66	+.22	+68.4
p	8.74	+.02	-4.2/B	+8.90/C	+29.20/B	260	Energy	9.47	+.31	+21.9/D	NS	NS	4	ValueA	17.07	+.02	+30.1
p	8.36	+.01	-5.8/D	+5.90/E	+24.70/D	121	EnergySer n	7.37	+.45	+60.9/A	NS	NS	23	**Selected Funds:**
Lp	8.43	+.02	-4.5/B	+9.50/B	+26.90/B	710	FinclSrv n	7.80	-.49	-18.0/E	NS	NS	22	AmShs p	34.37	-.86	+14.7
p	8.33	+.01	-4.9/C	+8.70/E	+23.50/E	88	HithCre n	9.98	+.02	-10.8/E	NS	NS	28	SplShs p	15.22	-.51	+14.9
Lp	8.49	+.02	-4.5/T	+7.90/D	+26.30/C	181	Juno n	9.40	-.19	+10.7/A	+4.30/C		16	**Seligman Group:**
IA p	97.30	-.73	+86.0/B	+162.70/B	+300.30/A	18,257	Nova n	35.94	-1.65	+8.8/D	+80.10/B	+289.80/A	567	CapFdA t	29.37	+.86	+75.3
IA p	10.63	-.24	-11.0/C	+5.50/E	+80.90/D	318	OTC n	87.88	-.12	+105.2/A	+344.50/A	+860.20/A	2,884	CapFdB p	26.46	+.77	+74.0
A p	8.17	+.02	-4.2/B	+8.60/C	+25.10/D	1,305	PrecMetls n	4.50	-.03	+3.2/C	-46.90/C	-39.50/C	39	CapFdD t	26.48	+.77	+74.0
A p	8.30	+.01	-4.9/C	+8.00/D	+27.80/B	133	Retailing n	11.12	-1.28	-10.9/D	NS	NS	46	COMuniA	6.77	+.02	-5.6
A p	44.57	+.36	+197.0/A	+233.90/A	+423.40/A	6,283	Tech n	27.76	-.38	+75.9/E	NS	NS	151	CmStkA t	13.50	-.37	-3.9
p	8.29	+.01	-4.9/C	+6.90/E	+25.00/D	159	Telecomm n	18.88	-.65	+46.0/C	NS	NS	48	CmStkB p	13.42	-.37	-4.3
p	8.36	+.02	-5.3/D	+6.10/E	+24.80/D	148	Transport	5.55	+.06	-28.7/E	NS	NS	3	CmStkD t	13.43	-.37	-4.3
irchA p	16.98	-.48	+17.1/B	+83.30/A	NS	682	USGvBd n	8.92	+.18	-10.5/E	+11.90/D	+39.00/D	31	ComunA t	51.06	-.92	+97.7
oValA p	10.00	+.43	NS	NS	NS	74	Ursa n	8.54	+.26	-4.3/D	-32.90/D	-55.00/D	388	ComunB t	46.86	-.86	+96.2
A p	7.22	+.02	+2.4/B	+8.30/E	NS	121	**SAFECO Funds:**							CommunC t	46.83	-.85	N
Lp	8.30	...	-4.7/B	+8.50/C	+26.30/C	1,595	BalancdA n	10.90	-.17	-4.6/E	+15.80/E		16	CommunD t	46.82	-.86	+96.3
p	14.01	+.03	-4.6/C	+7.50/D	+25.80/C	236	CalTFr n	11.02	+.04	-9.6/E	+8.50/E	+29.70/B	59	FLMuniA	7.15	+.02	-5.0
A	13.25	...													16.80	-.20	+45.2
EqA	10.46	-.03													18.11	-.21	+46.4
A p	12.15	+.05													16.81	-.20	+45.2
)	12.30	-.20													7.31	+.02	-5.2
p	19.44	+.52													14.53	-.43	+44.1
p	31.70	-.41													14.02	-.42	+43.0
)	41.14	-.18													20.68	+.03	+47.8
m Funds B:															19.55	+.02	+46.4
v t	8.15	+.04													33.59	-.69	+141.9
3 t	8.51	+.02													31.73	-.66	+140.2
t	17.50	-.47													8.36	-.03	+25.8
B t	12.41	-.20													9.23	-.38	+74.5
B t	10.34	-.02													8.97	-.38	+73.2
iB t	14.60	-.15													7.40	-.04	+24.8
t t	9.22	-.08	-5.1/E	+14.20/E	NA	172	SCFEmrgA	13.31	-.59	+63.6/E	NS	NS	43	EmgGD1	8.98	-.37	+73.4
3 t	7.99	+.01	-5.0/C	+8.90/D	+24.70/D	556	**SEI Asset Alloc:**							GibGroB t	14.02	-.41	+43.2
)r t	25.72	+.02	+20.6/B	+53.80/C	+167.00/B	1,178	ConservA n	11.17	-.07	+5.8/D	+34.20/C	NS	43	GloSmCB t	19.53	+.02	+46.4
)p p	11.07	+.34	+52.3/A	NS	NS	817	ConsIncA n	11.25	-.02	+3.9/D	+27.40/D	NS	31	GITechB t	31.77	-.66	+140.2
3 t	19.81	-.03	+18.8/B	+53.50/C	+143.00/C	278	GlGrwthA n	14.40	-.25	+19.6/A	+49.70/A	NS	108	GrowthB p	7.40	-.04	+24.8
3 t	10.61	+.04	+1.5/C	+5.20/E	+32.90/E	1,571	GlModGrA n	12.86	-.16	+14.6/E	+41.20/D	NS	46	HiYBdA p	6.22	-.04	-5/
lkt t	11.24	+.01	+89.1/B	+16.10/B	NS	62	GlobStkA n	14.77	-.33	+24.1/D	+57.60/C	NS	98	IntlA	22.39	-.26	+27.6
t	12.44	-.27	-9.0/D	+17.60/D	+93.70/C	548	ModGroA n	13.55	-.15	+9.8/B	+44.30/B	NS	180	HiYIdB t	6.22	-.04	-1.2
)t	26.69	-.24	+27.9/D	+81.90/C	+171.50/B	866	ModGroD p	13.47	-.15	+8.8/B	+40.30/B	NS	37	HiYIdBdC t	6.22	-.04	N
t	8.61	+.02	-5.1/C	+6.20/E	+22.50/E	73	USStkA n	16.60	-.35	+13.0/C	+65.00/B	NS	91	HiYIdBdD t	6.22	-.04	-1.4
it	15.07	-.19	-8.4/E	+15.40/E	+74.70/E	1,399	USStockD p	16.18	-.34	+11.9/C	+60.10/C	NS	42	IncomeB t	12.79	-.15	-5.6
it	11.42	...	-5.7/D	-4.80/E	+20.00/E	26	**SEI Portfolios:**							IncomeA	12.85	-.15	-4.9
B t	18.38	-.35	+58.7/B	+120.60/A	+240.40/A	832	BalancdA n	11.22	-.15	+2/E	+35.80/C	+96.60/C	49	IncomeD t	12.79	-.15	-5.6
t	17.42	-.35	+62.8/B	+122.00/A	+215.90/B	2,404	BndInxA n	9.98	+.05	-5/C	+16.10/B	+38.70/B	65	IntlB p	21.05	-.25	+26.8
I p	7.34	+.01	+2.7/C	NS	NS	817	CAMuniA n	9.84	-.01	-7/A	NS	NS	103	Intl t	21.04	-.25	+26.8
IncB t	12.56	-.13	+7.2/E	NS	NS	31	CapApA n	10.24	-.21	+3.0/E	+58.00/D	+160.50/D	58	LCapVaIA	8.44	-.15	-13.3
s t	17.95	+.34	+82.9/D	+11.30/B	+64.00/C	129	CoreFxInA n	9.82	+.05	-.7/D	+15.80/B	+40.90/A	2,525	LCapVID t	8.31	-.15	-13.9
t	16.49	-.46	-9.7/E	+16.90/E	+96.60/E	12,267	CorpDtA	1.97	...	+3.8/A	+16.50/A	+32.40/C	115	LCapVIB p	8.31	-.15	-13.9
3 t	10.93	-.26	-12.0/E	+12.00/E	NA	1,226	EmMktDbt n	8.82	+.03	+33.6/A	NS	NS	353	LAMuniA	7.52	+.02	-4.7
iB t	28.37	-1.04	+41.1/B	+145.90/A	NS	2,741	EmgMkt np	12.78	-.48	+82.9/C	-.40/D	+24.60/E	1,170	MassMuniA	7.15	+.03	-7.2
	67.53	+3.17	+14.4/D	+62.80/D	+182.30/C	2,197	EqIncA n	12.34	-.14	-5.5/C	+28.40/B	+108.30/B	51	MDMuniA	7.56	+.02	-3.8
Itx	10.22	-.05	+4.6/B	+8.00/D	+41.40/C	518	EqIndxA n	41.75	-1.26	+10.0/A	+71.40/A	+202.80/A	1,930	MIMuniA	7.84	+.03	-3.9
/B tx	7.71	-.03	+4.2/B	+4.80/E	+35.20/E	745	GNMA A n	9.21	+.01	-.4/D	+14.90/D	+37.90/A	84	MinnMuniA	7.10	+.02	-4.5
aB tx	6.29	...	-1.8/D	+8.10/E	+29.30/E	431	HiYld n	9.98	+.01	+2.3/C	+18.30/B	+59.80/A	515	MOMuniA	7.04	+.03	-5.7
3 t	4.75	+.01	+.3/E	+12.90/D	+31.80/D	120	IntMuniA	10.51	+.01	-1.6/A	+11.10/A	+28.00/B	707	NatlMuniA	7.40	+.03	-5.3
	29.83	-.80	+83.0/B	+119.40/A	+204.90/A	2,966	IntDGovA n	9.62	+.02	+.4/D	+15.70/A	+36.10/A	114	NJMuniA	6.83	+.02	-5.8
t	11.57	+.01	+22.4/E	+52.70/C	NS	459	IntlEqA n	14.11	-.31	+39.5/C	+65.00/B	+100.30/C	3,336	NYMuniA	7.45	+.03	-5.8
)t	25.23	-.09	+115.8/A	+143.30/A	NS	1,649	IntlFixA n	10.25	-.05	-6.9/D	+8.00/B	+26.10/D	896	NCMuniA	7.26	+.02	-5.3
rt	31.23	+.61	+136.8/A	+232.30/A	NS	480	LgCGroA n	33.72	-.79	+26.5/D	+119.40/B	NA	3,494	OhioMuniA	7.38	+.02	-4.6
	16.96	-.53	+19.7/D	+95.20/D	+239.60/C	4,087	LgCValA n	16.30	-.40	-7.5/D	+26.90/C	+116.50/C	2,888	ORMuniA	7.19	+.01	-4.6
t	8.73	+.01	-4.7/C	+6.80/E	+25.00/D	112	MidCapA n	15.28	...	+14.1/C	+35.50/B	+125.10/B	34	PAMuniA	7.22	+.02	-5.4
t	8.35	+.01	-6.3/E	+4.00/E	NA	40	NJ Muni n	9.68	...	-1.6/A	NS	NS	33	CAMuniA	5.97	+.01	-5.4
t	8.31	+.02	-5.5/D	+4.70/E	NA	46	NY Muni n	8.60	+.01	-2.2/A	NS	NS	30	CAMuQiA	6.13	+.02	-6.2
t	8.42	+.01	-5.1/C	+7.50/D	+25.10/D	426	PA MuniA n	10.08	+.02	-1.6/A	+11.00/A	+27.90/B	84	SCMuniA	7.33	+.03	-5.6
t	8.48	+.02	-5.1/C	+5.80/E	+22.20/C	87	S&P500A n	41.65	-1.26	+9.7/B	+70.50/B	NS	869	SCapVaIA	7.42	-.08	+2.1
pB t	91.92	-.70	+84.9/B	+157.30/B	+315.20/B	11,905	SmGovA n	9.88	+.01	+2.7/B	+16.30/A	+34.10/A	100	SCapValB p	7.28	-.07	+1.2
p	10.54	-.25	-11.8/E	+3.00/E	NS	315	SmCGroA n	32.83	+.35	+112.8/B	+130.70/C	+282.60/B	334	SCapValD p	7.28	-.07	+1.2
3 t	8.15	+.01	-4.9/C	+8.50/E	+21.10/E	180	SmCValA n	13.19	-.13	-1.7/E	-6.90/D	NA	610	US GvtA p	6.48	+.04	-2.5
)t	8.30	+.02	-5.4/D	+6.10/E	NA	52	TaxMgdLC	12.47	-.40	-5.5/E	NS	NS	1,123	US GovtBt	6.47	+.04	-3.2
it	41.96	+.35	+194.9/A	+226.50/B	+404.80/A	2,846	**SG Cowen Funds:**							US GovbD p	6.47	+.03	-3.2
t	8.28	+.01	-5.5/C	+4.90/E	+21.00/C	52	IncGrA p	9.69	...	-3.9/C	+8.10/E	+60.70/E	30	SenbancFd p	8.94	+.04	N
B t	8.35	+.02	-5.9/D	+4.00/E	+20.80/E	80	IFxdIncA p	8.92	-.01	-2.5/E	+12.00/E	+31.70/E	4	**Sentinel Group:**
rohB t	16.76	-.47	+16.3/B	NS	NS	730	LgCapValA p	9.66	-.08	+7.6/B	NS	NS	7	BalancedA p	17.57	-.16	-2.3
VIB p	9.95	+.42	NN	NN	NN	49	OpptA p	12.89	+.28	+43.9/A	+8.80/D	+49.70/E	19	BalancedB t	17.51	-.15	-3.0
3 t	7.23	+.02	+1.8/C	+8.00/E	NS	121	Opptl n	13.19	+.28	+44.2/A	+9.80/D	NA	9	BondA p	5.86	+.04	-1.5
t	8.30	...	-5.2/C	+8.50/D	+22.40/E	200	SIFE Trust	4.50	-.24	-19.4/E	+5.60/B	+110.00/A	726	ComStk A p	38.43	-.75	-4.4
3 t	13.28	+.01	-5.0/C	+7.50/D	+23.90/D	521	**SM&R Funds:**							ComS B t	36.35	-.76	-5.1
t	14.03	+.03	-4.9/C	+7.50/D	+24.40/D	273	Balan T	20.10	-.17	+12.6/A	+37.20/C	+92.40/C	29	GvSecsA p	9.45	+.06	-1.4
qB	10.42	-.04	NN	NN	NN	17	EqInc T	23.15	-.36	-8.4/D	+18.20/D	+76.90/E	170	GrthIndexA p	21.25	-.68	N
3 t	12.10	+.05	-1.1/E	+11.40/E	+30.90/E	862	GrowthT	8.34	-.11	+21.7/B	+58.70/C	+138.50/D	214	HiYIdA p	9.20	+.02	+3.2
	12.22	-.21	+1.8/C	+34.60/E	+97.60/D	452	**SSgA Funds:**							HiYIdB t	9.19	+.02	+2.6
t	18.11	+.48	+73.0/D	+130.50/C	+300.70/D	11,481	ActIntl	11.64	-.18	+31.5/D	+32.90/E	NS	106	MidCpGrA p	23.43	+.72	+67.4
	29.14	-.38	+59.8/C	+131.00/C	+266.50/C	11,481	BdMkt np	9.44	+.04	-.8/D	+15.10/A	NS	289	MidCpGrB p	22.86	+.70	+65.6
	39.66	-.16	+95.8/B	+175.80/B	NS	1,531	EmgMkt n	13.00	-.42	+70.2/D	+13.90/C	+57.20/B	406	PA TFA p	11.96	+.05	-4.8
m Funds C:							GrIncm n	22.99	-.58	-12.7/C	+90.40/A	+220.20/A	390	SMGvA p	9.47	+.02	+2.6
Cp	12.33	-.20	+14.7/B	+38.30/C	NA	133	HiYIdBd n	10.28	+.02	+5.3/A	NS	NS	38	SMGvD p	5.76	+.06	+33.5
Cp	14.47	-.15	+22.4/B	+51.90/B	NS	126	IAM Shares	10.20	-.31	NS	NS	NS	64	SmIC0B t	5.48	+.06	+34.2
nc	16.55	-.01	NN	NN	NN	40	Intm	9.29	+.03	+.5/A	+14.60/B	+36.20/C	59	TF IncA p	12.43	+.04	-4.2
clIC p	11.00	-.28	-12.3/E	NS	NS	32	IntlGrOpp p	15.13	-.11	+59.8/B	NS	NS	183	WorldA p	19.78	-.21	+22.2
pC p	28.73	-1.05	+41.3/B	NS	NS	144	LS Bal p	13.59	-.12	+11.5/A	NS	NS	117	WorldB t	19.57	-.21	+21.1
IC p	30.36	-.81	NN	NN	NN	39	LS Gro p	14.57	-.20	+15.9/B	NS	NS	61	SentryFd n	13.75	-.38	-9.1
	17.78	-.55	NN	NN	NN	61											

Getting Started

What is long-term day trading?

As noted in the introduction, long-term day trading is a combination of two investment strategies: long-term investing and short-term trading. Long-term investors prefer to buy and hold stocks for a long time, usually longer than 12 months. Their strategy is to make money by investing in the long-term prospects of a company. When the company does well, increasing profits and earnings, the price of the stock goes up. A common long-term strategy might be buying stock in an undervalued company for the lowest price possible and holding it until the stock returns to its fair market value. A successful buy-low, sell-high strategy is the dream of most long-term investors.

For investors, the fundamentals of a company, such as P/E (price/earnings) ratios, how the company is managed, or earnings, are the most important factors to consider. Because they care about the future growth and profitability of a company and its stock, investors analyze the fundamentals to determine the best stocks to buy and hold.

Short-term traders, on the other hand, don't want to hold their stocks for a long time. They want to make money as quickly as possible, preferably on a daily basis. For these traders, it isn't important to know about a company's CEO or its long-term potential. Short-term traders use a variety of technical charts to determine which stocks to buy or sell, rather than depending on fundamental data about a company. If they interpret the charts accurately, they can make money by selling when others are buying and buying when others are selling. They might hold a position overnight, for a few days, or perhaps for a few weeks (unlike many intra-day traders).

Which strategy do you prefer? Would you rather buy a stock and hold it for a long time, waiting until the price rises to make a profit? Or would you rather generate small, consistent profits and cash flow on a daily or very short-term basis?

The good news is that you don't have to limit yourself to one investment strategy. We believe you can—and should—use both. By combining long-term investment strategies with those of short-term traders, you can become what we call a long-term day trader and increase your overall profits in the market. A long-term day trader, therefore, is simply a long-term investor who uses the successful short-term strategies and tactics of day traders to improve investment returns.

You are probably familiar with the concept of buying stocks and holding them for the long term, but you may not be as familiar with day trading. For this reason, we'd like to give you a very brief overview.

The emergence of the online trader

Until just a few years ago, the only way you could trade stocks was by picking up the phone and calling your stockbroker. If you needed a quote on a stock, you'd call your broker. If you wanted information about a company, you'd call your broker. If you wanted to buy or sell a stock, you'd have to call your broker. Commissions were extremely high and customers were often plagued with slow execution of orders and lack of personal service.

The Internet, however, changed the investment world forever with the arrival of online brokers. With just the click of a mouse, a world of investment and stock information became available to the general public and leveled the playing field between individual investors and professional stockbrokers. Instead of relying on a broker to tell you what to buy or sell, you can now go online and do your own research, share ideas with other investors, get analysts' opinions, make your own trades, and save money on commissions. Many online tools offer consumers more information than most brokers have at their fingertips—and at no charge. Access to earnings estimates, company news, SEC filings, and information on insider selling are instantly available on the Internet.

And it's not expected to stop anytime soon. According to a survey by the Internet research firm Gomez Advisors and the polling firm Harris Interactive, more than 3.5 million people plan to open online trading accounts over the next six months. This means the online investing population is expected to swell to more than 9 million during the next year.

The Internet's increasing popularity has changed the stock market in other ways as well. Large numbers of new companies, such as Yahoo!, Cisco Systems, America Online, Tellabs, eBay, Amazon.com, and Dell Computer, have entered the market and experienced unprecedented growth. Prices of these new tech stocks can rise and fall by as much as 10 to 15 percent—and sometimes more—during the course of one trading day. For example, Qualcomm gained more than 150 points in one day. Imagine. If you had owned only 100 shares of Qualcomm at that time, you would have made a $15,000 profit in just one day (1 point equals $1).

It didn't take long for savvy investors to realize they could take advantage of these extreme price fluctuations. People began to buy and sell stocks repeatedly throughout a day, trying to profit from the rapid movement of a stock's price. Some traders would make dozens of trades a day, then sell all their stock positions at the end of the trading day when the market closed.

Others traded only one stock all day, riding it up and down for huge profits. Day trading rapidly caught the imagination of people everywhere, beginning what some have called a day-trading frenzy, thanks to the unprecedented rise in stock prices and especially to the rise in Internet stocks. It seemed as though everyone was making big bucks in the market by day trading stocks. It's no wonder that more than 250,000 people are trading stocks from the comfort of their homes on a part-time or full-time basis. Many of these people use online accounts to make short-term trades.

There are, however, some misconceptions about day trading that have made it seem extremely glamorous and fun. People picture themselves getting up in the morning and drinking coffee, possibly in their pajamas while reviewing trades from the previous day. Then, they think, they would study the market for a while, perhaps make a few trades, and then lock in a nice profit before noon by selling all their positions. After a leisurely lunch, they'll do a few more trades, making more money in a day than they used to in a month. Perhaps, they think, they'll retire in a few years. And best of all, they'll be their own bosses, free to make as much or as little money as they want. It sure seems like an easy way to make a living.

Not as easy as it sounds

The truth is that day trading is not as glamorous or as easy as many people think. First of all, most online day traders don't make huge profits on a consistent basis. The authors of the most popular day-trading books readily admit how few day traders actually make money. All you have to do is read the statistics: It is estimated that more than 75 percent of day traders lose money, especially when they are first starting out. This estimate includes both home-based online traders and those who work at day-trading firms. Although it looks easy when explained in a book by an enthusiastic writer, day trading is no place for amateurs. Even some pros have trouble making a consistent living buying and selling stocks within seconds or minutes.

The statistics are even worse for those who use intra-day trading strategies, sometimes called "trading the teenies" or "scalping." To make money on the teenies, you make your money on the spread, that is, the difference between the bid and ask price. (The bid is the price buyers are willing to pay for a stock, and the ask, or offer, is what sellers are willing to accept for it.) When you trade the teenies, your objective is to lock in small profits many times over throughout the day. It is estimated that more than 90 percent of intra-day traders lose money primarily due to commissions and poor money management. Because of poor fills and fast markets, a trader may face a multiple-point loss in a position. For example, it takes many 1/16- and 1/8-point profits to make up for a 4-point loss. Many unlucky traders have discovered that it's hard to be successful in the land of 1/16s and 1/8s.

Some critics call these day traders scalpers because they are trading for small profits. Although you probably won't make more than a few hundred dollars on each trade, if trades are made dozens of times throughout the day, your profits gradually mount. The traders who trade the teenies must depend on extremely fast execution times for their orders to survive.

Although you can often make significant profits trading the teenies, it is also easy to lose money. Because intra-day traders try to make profits on small movements in stock prices, they have to trade relatively large numbers of shares. To do this, they first need enough capital to make significant stock purchases, at least $25,000 to $50,000 to start. When they need additional capital, intra-day traders also tend to buy on margin to increase their buying power. Margin is like a huge credit card that allows one to borrow money from a brokerage firm to buy additional shares of stock.

If you are on the right side of a trade, you can do well using margin to increase your profits. If, however, you don't cut your losses in time, you could owe a huge amount of money to your brokerage. Intra-day traders defend the use of margin by stressing that they almost never hold an overnight position. Intra-day traders on margin who hold an overnight position could lose a fortune if the stock turned against them after the market closed. When you're on margin, even small losses can snowball against you. Therefore, if you do go on margin to trade, it is essential that you follow extremely strict money management rules.

Another difficulty with intra-day trading is that you are trading against some of the top pros in the business, pros who make a living beating individual investors. If you are going to be a successful intra-day trader, you must be a highly skilled technician. That is why the failure rate for this type of trading is so high. To make matters worse, many professional day traders who work on Wall Street don't like competition from retail traders and do everything in their power to confuse them.

One of the keys to being a successful day trader is to have or make enough money to keep trading. Professional traders will tell you that day trading is no different than running any other business. You need a business plan and trading capital as well as the technical knowledge and psychological disposition to run a successful business. Remember that the failure rate for startup companies is high—more than 50 percent each year. And, as you know, the statistics are much worse for beginning day traders. Under-capitalization is often cited as the reason for the failure of most startup companies. Likewise, lack of cash flow is the reason many day traders cannot sustain their activities.

Why do people tend to lose money day trading?

The answer, we believe, is a combination of unwise day-trading strategies, lack of knowledge, and lack of the discipline necessary to manage trades effectively. In our opinion, it doesn't make sense to risk $50,000 on a chance to make a couple of hundred dollars. The risk-reward levels are off the scale—that is, too much risk for too little reward. We came up with a short formula to help you understand this concept: The risks you take must be equal to or less than the profits you make.

Day-trading expenses are also high, averaging 56 percent a year according to one report. Commissions are the largest expense, followed by quote and data fees. Because day traders need to pay close attention to the market and need access to information quickly, there are costs for access to live, immediate quotes and other real-time data. All of these costs make it very difficult and expensive to succeed.

Finally, day trading takes an almost supernatural amount of discipline, knowledge, and intuition to be successful. The most successful traders work long hours learning and developing new strategies. Most people just don't have the psychological makeup it takes to be a successful day trader.

Day-trading firms

Day trading first became popular in offices called SOES shops, which were so named because their traders were taking advantage of the NASDAQ Small Order Execution System (SOES), which instantaneously filled orders at the best prices. Today, because of the advent of online trading, most day traders work out of their homes. Still, for a high monthly fee and minimal startup capital of between $25,000 and $50,000, you can work in a room with dozens of other traders at a day-trading firm, where you will have several advantages.

Most important, the firm will provide you with the most sophisticated computer hardware and customized trading software on the market. Day-trading firms usually have multiple T1 lines and servers connected directly to the exchange. This will give you an edge if you are making dozens of trades every day. Firms also offer low commissions, fast trade execution, and access to Level II screens, which give you the most detailed quote information on individual stocks.

Another advantage of a day-trading firm is that you can make your trades in the company of other traders. With luck, you will improve by studying how successful traders in the firm buy and sell. Day-trading firms will also train you to use their software and teach you specific strategies that will help you make money in the market. In fact, many day-trading firms make more money on the educational programs they offer than on commissions.

On July 29, 1999, the day-trading community got a lot of un-wanted publicity when a disgruntled trader, Mark Barton, burst into the offices of two day-trading firms in Atlanta with a gun, shooting 14 traders and killing seven, many of them acquaintances and fellow traders. Some of the traders Barton killed had loaned him money to cover his huge trading losses. After losing more than $400,000 in seven months of day trading, Barton decided to end his own life, taking his family and as many day traders as he could with him. After a brief chase by police, Barton pulled his car into a gas station and killed himself.

As a result of Barton's rampage, the Securities and Exchange Commission (SEC) conducted a full-scale investigation of the prac-tices of day-trading firms. Although no more than 5,000 people day trade full-time at retail firms, the government wanted to know more about how these firms do business. They were especially interested in the margin requirements of day traders and whether day traders are encouraged to lend each other money to keep trading.

In response to these concerns, the National Association of Secu-rities Dealers (NASD) and the New York Stock Exchange (NYSE) pro-posed a new rule requiring day traders to have at least 50 percent cash in their accounts to cover potential losses. Day trading is de-fined in the proposal as the buying and selling of stocks within one day. Many of the rule changes also affect "pattern day traders," those who make more than four "round-trip" trades on the same stock within a week. This apparently refers to the hundreds of thousands of elec-tronic day traders who place most of their trades from home. Because of the negative backlash against day trading, a number of day-trad-ing firms now refer to their customers as short-term traders rather than day traders.

The bottom line on day-trading firms is that when you add up the cost of the training courses, monthly access fees, and commis-sions and taxes, you will have to do spectacularly well to just break even. The odds are not in your favor, although some people have done very well.

What is short-term trading?

If it is so difficult to become a day trader and the term has developed such a negative connotation, you might wonder why we are recommending that you become one. Actually, we are recommending that you become a short-term trader, using a variety of short-term strategies to boost your returns. What we are saying is that intra-day trading, the strategy most people associate with day trading, should be avoided by most individual traders, even if it is used by some professionals. As noted earlier, intra-day trading involves buying and selling dozens of stocks within minutes or hours, often with the goal of making small 1/16- and 1/8-point profits. Only a handful of people have the temperament to be a successful intra-day trader. The best advice we can give you is to take the time to study all of the short-term strategies before you commit real money to the market.

One very profitable short-term strategy is swing trading, or holding stocks for one- to five-day periods. Although swing traders rely on many of the same technical indicators as intra-day traders, they aim for much higher gains—profits of a few points or more. Many of our most profitable trades have been swing trades, but we are careful to pick stocks only in high-quality companies, those we consider the market leaders. If you swing trade Internet stocks, however, you are substantially increasing your risk. That is why many risk-averse short-term traders prefer to trade many of the NYSE blue-chip stocks. They are still volatile but are much more predictable than many NASDAQ stocks. If you are new to short-term trading, you might want to stick with NYSE stocks, at least at first.

No matter what strategy you ultimately use, we can define short-term trading as simply a mechanism for increasing short-term profits and cash flow. It could mean entering and exiting a position within a few minutes, a few days, or even a few weeks. Most of the strategies in this book, however, are geared to buying and selling within one to five days. Long-term day traders will use a variety of short-term trading strategies and will also invest a portion of their portfolio in stocks, mutual funds, and index funds.

Long-term day trading: a diversified approach

When you become a long-term day trader, you will favor a more diversified approach to investing in the stock market. As you probably know, diversification is one of the most important concepts of financial planning. To diversify is to split your money among different types of investments, such as stocks, bonds, and cash. Most experts agree diversification is a very effective way of reducing overall investment risk. There are few investment advisors who believe you should put 100 percent of your money into one asset class. Although there is no way for you to control market risk, you can control investment risk, and one of the most effective ways of doing so is to diversify.

As long-term day traders, we believe strongly in diversification. In fact, the key to our philosophy is to diversify among a number of investments, as well as combine short-term and long-term strategies. If the market drops by more than 10 percent, for example, the damage shouldn't be severe if you are invested in stocks, mutual funds, and cash. You can also use the short-term portion of your portfolio to try and profit as the market begins to recover. No rule states you must choose between long- and short-term investments. We believe it makes sense to use both.

As a long-term day trader, you are minimizing risk by being diversified among long-term and short-term investments. We believe it is too risky to use short-term trading tactics with your entire portfolio. Leave that to the professionals, who are paid to trade with other people's money. The good news is that with short-term trading tactics you can make money regardless of the market direction. We will show you exactly how to make money on both the long and short side of the market. Even if the market goes down 10 or 15 percent, it is possible for you to make a profit.

If you are primarily a long-term investor, you should not be concerned with the short-term direction of the Dow Jones Industrial Average (DJIA or the Dow), an index comprised of 30 well-known companies listed on the NYSE. The long-term investor depends on the fact that over time the stock market tends to go up, although there are no guarantees. If history is any guide, long-term investors should do quite well over time. In this book, however, we will concentrate primarily on short-term strategies. As we said before, we think you can successfully use both strategies.

The advantages of being a long-term day trader

As a long-term day trader, you don't have to quit your full-time job to make money in the market. There is always the possibility you can find legitimate times during the day (perhaps at lunch or at breaks) to make short-term trades. This does not mean you should spend your entire lunch period buying and selling stocks while staring at your computer screen. What we hope to teach you is how to trade smarter, not necessarily to trade more.

Don't forget that some of the best short-term traders in the country are extremely selective about the trades they make. Contrary to popular belief, you don't have to make dozens of trades a day to make money. Over-trading is a serious problem for many traders. Try to spend more of your time analyzing trading opportunities than acting on them. Ultimately, you will be in a better position to profit when you are convinced the time is right for you to make a trade.

Nevertheless, no matter how much free time you have at the office, it is still not recommended that you buy or sell stocks while at work. We know from personal experience how difficult it is to trade stocks while working at a full-time job. If you spend more time checking up on the market than doing your job, you might have to find another place to work. If you have to make a choice between your full-time job and your short-term portfolio, stick with the job, at least until you are convinced you can make a full-time living as a trader.

Because of some remarkable changes happening on Wall Street, the good news is you might be able to keep your full-time job and still trade stocks. Now is actually the perfect time to be a long-term day trader. As you may have read in the newspapers or seen on television, it is now possible for you to place trades before the market opens or after it closes. Quite a few short-term traders are beginning to use the after-hours market to place their trades, and it is also catching on with the general public. Check with your online brokerage to find out how long it remains open and what stocks are being traded during this time.

Many professional traders believe the after-hours market will eventually be popular with the investing public. There is no need to let your full-time job get in the way of making money in the market; television channel CNBC closely monitors the after-hours market at the close of the regular market every day. Thanks to after-hours trading, it is possible for you to have income from two sources.

If you are self-employed, a stay-at-home parent, or if you work out of your home, you will find that short-term trading can be particularly convenient for you. You can trade stocks and still work out of the comfort of your own home—an ideal way to boost your income.

Long-term day trading also allows you to have more leisure time. Because you are protecting yourself from unexpected market corrections or other unanticipated events by diversifying among a number of investments, you don't have to worry about how the market is doing every minute. This doesn't mean you can ignore the movement of the stock market for long periods of time; it just means you don't have to spend the entire day staring obsessively at red and green computer screens like some career day traders.

As a long-term investor, you can invest in mutual funds, stocks, or cash without having to constantly monitor how your investments are doing. A number of popular long-term investment strategies involve a minimum of time. For busy people who don't have time to closely monitor their investments, long-term investing makes sense. It has been incredibly profitable for millions of people, especially in the middle of a bull market.

Long-term investors like David and Tom Gardner, the Motley Fool, have helped to educate retail investors about the importance of buying and holding stocks for the long term. They have provided their followers with a variety of long-term investment approaches, from conservative to highly aggressive portfolio. If you follow the Fool, and it has been remarkably successful, the key to success is buying quality stocks and holding them forever. The Gardners are strong believers in Warren Buffett's buy-and-hold philosophy, although the Fool often buys Internet companies. If you pick the stocks of profitable companies, your long-term investments tend to take care of themselves. It tends to be a passive but profitable strategy.

Because short-term trading is more aggressive than buy-and-hold investing, you will need to closely monitor your stocks and become more involved with your investments on a daily basis. Short-term traders cannot afford to keep their eyes away from the computer screen for too long. Although you don't have to watch the screen every second, you must pay very close attention to price movement, volume, and the strength or weakness of specific sectors.

In addition, if you are a novice short-term trader, you probably aren't going to be watching more than a dozen or so stocks at one time. This will give you time to conduct research and become more knowledgeable about technical analysis. Although it takes some time to learn the basics, technical analysis is worth learning, no matter what kind of investor you are.

Getting started

We don't think you need to join a day-trading firm, hire a stockbroker, or install customized software on your home computer to be a long-term day trader. You can get by with a high-speed modem connection, the Internet, and an online broker. (The faster your Internet connection, the more convenient it will be to trade.) Online broker commissions have gotten cheaper, execution times are faster, and you can trade at home or anywhere you find an Internet connection. Some people are trading stocks through a laptop computer or a wireless device.

With a high-speed modem connection, you can trade almost as fast as the pros without paying a fortune for new equipment. The brokerages that are connected to an Electronic Communication Network (ECN), and most of the major brokerages are, provide you with the fastest and most cost-effective service. For example, Datek Online, which routes its orders through the Island ECN, has free-streaming quotes and extremely fast execution times. Streaming quotes are automatically updated, which means you can monitor several stocks at one time.

Another popular online brokerage favored by many short-term traders is E*Trade. Like many of its competitors, E*Trade offers an array of investment services for both short-term traders and long-term investors.

Finally, the online brokerage with the most market share at the time of this writing, Charles Schwab, has traditionally been favored by long-term buy-and-hold investors. Although Schwab charges a bit more than the competition, it makes up for the price difference by providing many personalized services such as extensive research and 24-hour telephone service.

The hardest part of setting up an account with an online broker is deciding which one is best. There are more than 100 online brokers to choose from and more are popping up every day. You have probably noticed that even full-service brokerages have entered the lucrative online brokerage business.

Before you send a check to open up an account, be sure to compare the various fees and services. Some online brokerages give you unlimited free quotes, extremely low commissions, and telephone support. Your goal is to find a brokerage with the best customer service and fastest trade execution. Although price is important and you want to save money, you really must look at the whole package. A lot depends on your trading style. For example, if you rarely make trades but spend most of your time researching, then the higher commission charges at Charles Schwab and Merrill Lynch won't concern you because they offer you so much research.

On the other hand, if you are an aggressive, experienced short-term trader, you might want a no-frills online brokerage with low commissions, fast order handling, and minimal computer failures. Keep in mind that most online brokerages are still Web-based systems, which means that after you press the Enter key, your order is routed or passed off to a middleman, most likely a market maker or specialist, who executes it. Most professional day traders, however, buy special software that allows them to bypass the online brokerage and send their order directly to an ECN or a market maker. Expect to pay your local day-trading firm a fee for the direct-access software and equipment. It really is up to you to determine whether an online brokerage or direct access will meet your needs.

Before you sign on the dotted line, spend a few hours doing research. One of the fastest ways to determine which brokerage will meet your needs is to visit its Web site. Most have user-friendly, interactive Web sites with loads of investment information. Another way to learn more about online brokerages and find out which is best for your needs is to call the customer service department. The members of the department should be eager to answer all of your questions. If they can't help you before you become a customer, it is unlikely that they will help you afterwards. Also, be on the lookout for feature articles from major financial magazines such as *Barron's*, *Kiplinger's*, *Money*, *Individual Investor*, *Smart Money*, *Worth*, and *Bloomberg Personal Finance*, which routinely compare and contrast all the online brokerages. Finally, don't forget that one of the most effective ways to find an online brokerage is through word of mouth. We suggest you find out the information you need from friends who are experienced investors rather than following the advice of strangers in a chat room.

What equipment do you need?

A long-term day trader doesn't necessarily need specialized computer equipment, although all online traders should have a high-end computer, such as a Pentium III Gateway, Dell, or Compaq, although there are dozens more to choose from, including Apple computers. The goal is to have the most efficient equipment available to allow you to process your trades as quickly as possible, no matter what your style of trading. You don't necessarily need a top-of-the-line computer to be an online trader, but having one usually means you will get such state-of-the-art components as large hard drives, fast modems, and lots of RAM.

Many online traders bought the most technologically advanced computers on the market, equipped with fast internal 56k V.90 modems. Imagine their surprise when they discovered they were still connecting to the Internet at relatively sluggish 28k- or 31k-baud rates. Why? Because no matter how fast your internal modem, you are slowed down by the speed of your existing telephone line.

The good news for traders is that the market for improved communication lines is about to explode, giving consumers faster Internet access at much lower prices. The major players—local telephone carriers, cable companies, and Internet providers—are all vying for a chance to give you split-second Internet access. As more people depend on the Internet to conduct business, they will demand faster access speeds for reasonable prices. Anyone who can meet the needs of consumers for faster Internet access will likely reap billions in the near future. If you don't have the time or money to upgrade your existing telephone lines to the latest telecommunication network, be sure you have an internal or external 56k V.90 analog modem installed on your computer. By the time you are ready to upgrade, the telecommunication technology will likely be faster and cheaper.

If, however, you need immediate access to the Internet and you don't want to wait months to find out who is going to provide the fastest, lowest cost service, you have several choices. You can start with the up-and-coming DSL technology, which allows both analog and digital Internet connections. It is extremely fast and best of all, you don't have to install a second line in your house to use it. Unfortunately, DSL technology isn't widely available, although some DSL modems, specifically ADSL, should be shipped in large quantities during the next year. A second choice is to install a cable modem, which is convenient, reasonably priced, and much faster than a standard analog modem, although not as fast as ADSL. Another choice is ISDN, an all-digital telecommunication network that has been around for years. With the increased competition from DSL and cable technology, it is unknown how long ISDN will last.

Finally, if you own your own business and need instantaneous Internet access without regard to price, you could install a T1 line. Most day-trading firms have T1 lines installed, but the price is exorbitant, well beyond the reach of most individual investors.

Level I and Level II screens

Many long-term day traders can trade successfully using standard Level I screens, the type most online brokerages provide their customers. With Level I screens, you get basic information about a stock, including the bid and ask price, volume, the 52-week high or low, and P/E ratios. Most brokerages give you real-time stock updates. A few online brokerages, for example, Datek Online, E*Trade, DLJ Direct, and Fidelity, provide customers streaming quotes, which give you streaming updated real-time quotes.

Most short-term traders, especially professional day traders, pay for Level II screens, which give them additional information about NASDAQ stocks, including the best bid and ask price, inside quotes, and volume. The color-coded Level II screens give the pros important clues about the stocks the NASDAQ market makers are buying and selling and in what quantities. Many day-trading pros depend on Level II trading screens to successfully compete in the market. Only the fastest and most informed day traders make money, and Level II screens can give them the edge they need.

One of the most useful features of a Level II screen is its ability to let the user see the "inside" market. On a Level I screen, all you see is the bid and ask price of a stock. Let's say the bid price is 10 1/2 and the ask price is 11. With a Level I screen, all you know is that you could buy the stock at 11 and sell it at 10 1/2. But there could be hundreds of other buyers and sellers who are willing to buy and sell at prices inside the listed bid and ask price. A Level II screen shows you this inside market. If you are an intra-day trader trying to profit from 1/8s and 1/16s of a point, you should have a Level II screen.

Although Level II screens are an extremely valuable tool, they are very expensive and not required for long-term day traders. The strategy of reading market makers using Level II screens is difficult and time-consuming. According to some market makers, the narrowing of spreads between the bid and ask price on NASDAQ stocks has made it extremely hard for them to make huge profits. It is naive to think that a day trader can jump in with nothing but a Level II screen and consistently beat the market makers at their own game. It is true, however, that a professional day trader can get valuable clues from the Level II screen. The bottom line for long-term day traders: You can be profitable without using Level II screens. Although the information they provide is valuable, a lot depends on how much time you're going to devote to trading. If this is going to be your full-time job, Level II screens are a requirement. If you're going to trade part-time, you can do without it.

Summary

To summarize, a long-term day trader is an investor who buys and holds certain stocks for a long period but who also uses the successful short-term strategies and tactics of day traders to make money in the market. We don't believe that you should limit yourself to one investment strategy. In fact, we propose that you have two strategies, one long-term and one short-term. It also makes sense to open up two brokerage accounts so you can keep track of and compare the portfolios from both trading strategies.

There is absolutely nothing wrong with the long-term buy-and-hold strategy, and we agree that everyone should invest a significant portion of his or her assets in stable, long-term investments. Because of the growth of the U.S. economy, there is a good chance for excellent investment returns over the next five, 10, or possibly 20 years. For those people who have a long investment time horizon, long-term investing can be a very successful way to create future wealth. This strategy has worked remarkably well for millions of people, especially employees who contribute to 401(k) plans and other payroll deduction plans.

Day trading, however, can provide you with an opportunity to make money in the short term without waiting years to see the results. While your long-term portfolio is dependent on the belief that with time the market tends to go up, day trading allows you to take advantage of the current, short-term market environment. You must never forget that although our stock market has done extremely well during the last 60 years, there is no guarantee the good times will continue. All you have to do is look at Japan to see that things don't always turn out the way the experts predict.

Japan's Nikkei average went as high as 38,957 in December 1989, until a series of devastating financial errors by the government sent Japan into an eight-year recession. As of January 2000, Japan was still 50 percent below those all-time highs. Although a short-term strategy will not completely protect you from a major correction or bear market, if used wisely, it can help you make money in virtually any market condition. One of the most valuable lessons in this book is the rule on shorting stocks, which teaches you how to profit when everyone else is selling.

We hope we've made it clear that most people should avoid trading the teenies or scalping. This kind of day trading is a game best played by the pros and involves an incredible amount of time and capital. If you are truly interested in buying and selling stocks within the same day, there are a number of excellent books on the subject. However, we believe you will have the best chance to make consistent profits over time by being a long-term day trader.

On to the rules

Now that you have a better idea of what long-term day trading is, it's time to reveal a few of our secrets. In Section II, we show you how to become a successful short-term trader. Our goal is to help you use the strategies and tactics of short-term traders to boost your daily, weekly, or yearly returns.

▶ Section II ◀
Short-Term Trading Rules

A px	7.74	-.04	+5.0/A	+7.20/E	+40.30/E	900
III p	7.33	+.01	+3.5/B	NS	NS	569
.px	6.33	+.01	-1.0/C	+8.50/E	+34.30/D	1,046
A p	4.74	+.01	+.6/D	+14.70/B	+35.50/A	230
p	30.46	-.81	+64.2/B	+124.30/A	+216.70/A	5,163
n p	11.69	+.01	+23.3/E	+56.00/C	NS	508
o p	27.07	-.10	+117.4/A	+148.90/A	+270.30/A	1,526
/ p	31.64	+.62	+138.7/A	+240.20/A	NS	650
	17.85	-.55	+20.6/D	+100.20/C	+254.00/C	7,619
p	8.74	+.02	-4.2/B	+8.90/C	+29.20/B	280
p	8.36	+.01	-5.8/D	+5.90/E	+24.70/D	121
p	8.43	+.02	-4.5/B	+9.50/B	+28.90/B	710
p	8.33	+.01	-4.9/C	+8.70/E	+23.50/C	88
A p	8.49	+.02	-4.5/B	+7.90/D	+26.30/C	181
A p	97.30	-.73	+86.0/B	+162.70/B	+330.30/B	18,257
A p	10.63	-.24	-11.0/E	+5.50/E	+80.90/D	318
A p	8.17	+.02	-4.2/B	+8.60/C	+25.10/D	1,305
A p	8.30	+.01	-4.9/C	+8.00/D	+27.80/B	133
p	44.57	+.38	+197.0/A	+233.80/A	+423.40/A	6,283
p	8.29	+.01	-4.9/C	+6.90/D	+25.00/D	159
	8.36	+.02	-5.3/D	+6.10/E	+24.80/D	148
rchA p	16.98	-.48	+17.1/B	+83.30/A	NS	682
IValA p	10.00	+.43	NS	NS	NS	74
A p	7.22	+.02	+2.4/B	NS	NS	23
p	8.30	...	-4.7/B	+8.50/C	+26.30/C	1,595
p	14.01	+.03	-4.4/B	+7.50/D	+25.80/C	236
A	13.25	...				
qA	10.46	-.03				
A p	12.15	+.05				
	12.30	-.20				
p	19.44	+.52				
D	31.70	-.41				
D	41.14	-.16				
m Funds B:						
v t	8.15	+.04				
3 t	8.51	+.02				
t	17.50	-.47				
B t	12.41	-.20				
3 t	10.34	-.02				
B t	14.60	-.15				

Rydex Investor:

Nova n	35.70	-1.55	+8.4/D	NS	NS	20
OTC n	87.27	-.13	+104.2/A	NS	NS	66
Ursa n	8.46	+.25	-4.9/D	NS	NS	4
Arktos n	3.94	...	-55.9/E	NS	NS	130
Banking n	6.12	-.45	-29.6/E	NS	NS	21
BasicMat n	7.70	+.02	+2.8/E	NS	NS	6
Biotech n	38.00	+6.94	+221.7/A	NS	NS	372
ElectInv n	33.79	+.18	+148.1/C	NS	NS	124
Energy	9.47	+.31	+21.9/D	NS	NS	4
EnergySer n	7.37	+.45	+80.9/A	NS	NS	13
FinclSrv n	7.80	-.49	-18.0/D	NS	NS	22
HlthCre n	9.96	+.02	-10.8/E	NS	NS	28
Juno n	9.40	-.19	+10.7/A	+4.30/C	NS	16
Nova n	35.94	-1.65	+8.8/D	+80.10/B	+269.80/A	567
OTC n	87.88	-.12	+105.2/A	+344.50/A	+860.20/A	2,884
PrecMetls n	4.50	-.03	+3.2/C	-46.90/C	-39.50/C	39
Retailing n	11.12	-1.26	-10.9/D	NS	NS	4
Tech n	27.76	-.38	+73.9/E	NS	NS	151
Telecomm n	18.88	-.65	+46.0/C	NS	NS	48
Transport	5.55	+.06	-28.7/E	NS	NS	5
USGvBd n	8.92	+.18	-10.5/E	+11.90/D	+39.00/D	31
Ursa n	8.54	+.26	-4.3/D	-32.90/D	-55.00/D	388

SAFECO Funds:

| Balanced n | 10.90 | -.17 | -4.8/E | +15.80/E | NS | 16 |
| CalTEr n | 11.02 | +.04 | -9.6/E | +6.50/E | +29.70/B | 81 |

| SCFEmrgA | 13.31 | -.59 | +63.6/E | +5.80/C | NS | 43 |

SEI Asset Alloc:

ConservA n	11.17	-.07	+5.8/D	+34.20/C	NS	43
ConaIncA n	11.25	-.02	-3.9/D	+27.40/D	NS	31
GlGrwthA n	14.40	-.25	+19.6/A	+49.70/A	NS	108
GlModGrA n	12.86	-.16	+14.6/A	+41.20/D	NS	46
GlobStkA n	14.77	-.33	+24.1/D	+57.60/C	NS	69
ModGroA n	13.55	-.15	+9.8/B	+44.30/B	NS	180
ModGroD p	13.47	-.15	+8.8/D	+40.30/B	NS	37
USStkA n	16.60	-.35	+13.0/C	+65.00/B	NS	91
USStockD p	16.18	-.34	+11.9/C	+60.10/C	NS	42

SEI Portfolios:

BalancdA n	11.22	-.15	+.2/E	+35.80/C	+86.60/C	49
BndInxA n	9.98	+.05	-.5/C	+16.10/B	+38.70/B	85
CAMuniA n	9.84	-.01	-.7/A	NS	NS	103
CapApA n	10.24	-.21	+3.0/E	+58.00/D	+160.50/D	58
CoreFxInA n	9.82	+.05	-.7/D	+15.80/B	+40.90/A	2,525
CorpDIA	1.97	...	+3.8/A	+16.50/A	+32.40/C	115
EmMktDbt n	8.92	+.03	+33.6/A	NS	NS	353
EmgMkt np	12.78	-.48	+82.9/C	-.40/D	+24.60/E	1,170
EqIncA n	8.34	-.14	-5.5/C	+28.40/B	+108.30/B	51
EqIndxA n	41.75	-1.26	+10.0/A	+71.40/A	+202.80/A	1,930
GNMA A n	9.21	+.01	-.4/D	+14.90/B	+37.90/A	84
HiYld n	9.98	+.01	+2.3/C	+18.30/B	+58.90/A	615
IntMuniA n	10.51	+.01	-1.6/A	+11.10/A	+28.00/D	707
IntDGovA n	9.62	+.02	+.4/D	+15.70/A	+36.10/A	114
IntEqA n	14.11	-.31	+39.5/C	+65.00/B	+100.30/C	2,336
IntlFixA n	10.25	-.05	-6.9/D	+8.90/B	+26.10/D	896
LgCGroA n	33.72	-.79	+28.5/D	+119.40/B	NS	3,494
LgCValA n	16.30	-.40	-7.5/D	+26.90/C	+116.50/B	2,888
MidCapA n	15.28	...	+14.1/C	+35.50/B	+125.10/B	34
NJ Muni n	9.68	...	-1.6/A	NS	NS	33
NY Muni n	9.60	+.01	-2.2/A	NS	NS	30
PA MuniA n	10.08	+.02	-1.6/A	+11.60/A	+27.90/B	84
S&P500A n	41.65	-1.26	+9.7/B	+70.50/B	NS	869
ShtGovA n	9.88	+.01	+2.7/B	+16.30/A	+34.10/A	100
SmCGroA n	32.83	+.35	+112.8/B	+130.70/C	+282.60/B	1,334
SmCValA n	13.19	-.13	-1.7/E	+6.90/D	NA	610
TaxMgdLC	12.47	-.40	+5.5/E	NS	NS	1,123

SG Cowen Funds:

IncGrA p	9.69	...	-3.9/C	+8.10/E	+60.70/E	30
IFxdIncA p	9.82	-.01	-2.5/E	+12.00/E	+31.70/E	4
LgCapValA p	9.68	-.08	+7.6/B	NS	NS	7
OpptA p	12.89	+.28	+43.9/A	+8.80/D	+49.70/E	19
Oppti n	13.19	+.28	+44.2/A	+9.80/D	NA	9
SIFE Trust	4.50	-.24	-19.4/E	+5.60/B	+110.00/B	726

SM&R Funds:

Balan T	20.10	-.17	+12.6/A	+37.20/C	+92.40/C	29
EqInc T	23.15	-.36	-6.4/D	+18.20/D	+76.90/C	179
GrowthT	6.34	-.11	+21.7/B	+58.70/D	+138.50/D	214

SSgA Funds:

ActIntl	11.64	-.18	+31.5/D	+32.90/C	NS	106
BdMkt np	9.44	+.04	-.6/B	+15.10/A	NS	289
EmgMkt n	13.00	-.42	+70.2/D	+13.90/C	+57.20/B	408
GrIncm n	22.99	-.58	+12.7/C	+90.40/A	+220.20/A	390
HiYldBd n	10.08	+.02	+5.3/A	NS	NS	38
IAM Shares	10.20	-.31	NS	NS	NS	64
Intrm	9.29	+.03	+.5/A	+14.60/B	+36.20/C	109
IntlGrOpp p	15.13	-.11	+59.8/B	NS	NS	89
LS Bal p	13.59	-.12	+15.1/B	NS	NS	117
LS Gro p	14.57	-.20	+15.9/B	NS	NS	61

Security Funds:

Bond p	6.44	+.03	-2.6
CapPresA p	10.00	...	...
Equity	9.79	-.32	+2.7
EquityB t	9.26	-.31	+1.6
EqGIA	19.76	+.06	+77.4
GrInc	8.06	-.11	-6.9
MuniBd	9.47	+.03	-4.1
Ultra	13.66	+.22	+88.4
ValueA	17.07	+.02	+30.1

Selected Funds:

| AmShs p | 34.37 | -.86 | +14.7 |
| SplShs p | 15.22 | -.51 | +14.9 |

Seligman Group:

CapFdA t	29.37	+.86	+75.3
CapFdB p	26.46	+.77	+74.0
CapFdD t	26.48	+.77	+74.0
COMuniA	6.77	+.02	-5.6
CmStkA t	13.50	-.37	-3.9
CmStckB p	13.42	-.37	-4.3
CmStckD t	13.43	-.37	-4.3
ComunA t	51.06	-.92	+97.7
ComunB t	48.86	-.86	+96.2
CommunC t	48.83	-.85	N
CommunD t	48.82	-.86	+96.3
ELMuniA	7.15	+.02	-5.0
	16.80	-.03	+45.2
	18.11	-.21	+46.4
	18.61	-.20	+45.2
	7.31	+.02	-5.2
	14.53	-.43	+44.1
	14.02	-.42	+43.0
	20.68	+.03	+47.8
	19.55	+.02	+46.4
	33.59	-.69	+141.9
	31.73	-.66	+140.2
	8.36	-.03	+25.8
	9.23	-.38	+74.5
	8.97	-.38	+73.2
GrowthD t	7.40	-.04	+24.8
EmgGD t	8.98	-.37	+73.4
GlbGroB t	14.02	-.41	+43.2
GloSmCB t	19.53	+.02	+46.4
GlTechB t	31.77	-.68	+140.2
GrowthB p	7.40	-.04	+24.8
HiYBdA p	6.22	-.04	-5.0
IntlA	22.39	-.28	+27.8
HiYBd B	6.22	-.04	-1.2
HiYldBdC t	6.22	-.04	N
HiYBdD t	6.22	-.04	-1.4
IncomeB t	12.79	-.15	-5.8
IncomeA	12.85	-.15	-4.9
IncomeD t	12.79	-.15	-5.8
IntlB p	21.05	-.25	+26.8
IntlD t	21.04	-.25	+26.8
LCapValA	8.44	-.15	-13.3
LCapVlD p	8.31	-.15	-13.9
LCapVlaB p	8.31	-.15	-13.9
LAMuniA	7.52	+.02	-4.7
MassMunlA	7.15	+.03	-7.2
MDMuniA	7.56	+.02	-3.8
MIMuniA	7.84	+.03	-3.9
MinnMuniA	7.10	+.02	-4.5
MOMuniA	7.04	+.03	-5.7
NatlMuniA	7.40	+.03	-5.3
NJMuniA	6.83	+.02	-5.8
NYMuniA	7.45	+.03	-5.8
NCMuniA	7.26	+.02	-5.3
OhioMuniA	7.38	+.02	-4.8
ORMuniA	7.19	+.01	-4.8
PAMuniA	7.22	+.02	-5.4
CAMuniA	5.97	+.01	-5.4
CAMuniQlA	6.13	+.02	-6.2
SCMuniA	7.33	+.03	-5.6
SCapValA p	7.42	-.08	+2.1
SCapValB p	7.28	-.07	+1.2
SCapValD p	7.28	-.07	+1.2
US GvtA p	6.46	+.04	-3.2
US GovtB t	6.47	+.04	-3.2
US GovD p	6.47	+.03	-3.2
SenbancFd p	8.94	+.04	N

Sentinel Group:

BalancedA p	17.57	-.16	-2.3
BalancedB t	17.61	-.15	-2.3
BondA p	5.86	+.04	-1.5
ComStk A p	38.43	-.75	-4.4
ComS B t	36.35	-.76	-5.1
GvSecsA p	9.45	+.06	-1.4
GrthIndexA	21.25	-.68	N
HiYldA p	9.20	+.02	+3.2
HiYldB t	9.19	+.02	+2.6
MdCpGrA p	23.43	+.72	+57.4
MidCpGrB p	22.84	+.70	+55.6
PA TFA p	11.96	+.05	-4.8
SMGvA p	9.47	+.02	+2.6
SmCoA p	5.76	+.06	+33.5
SmCoB t	5.48	+.06	+32.4
TF IncA p	12.43	+.04	-4.2
WorldA p	19.78	-.21	+22.9
WorldB t	19.57	-.21	+21.1
SentryFd n	13.75	-.38	-9.1

Short-Term Trading Rules

100101010010111
10111010101101
1010001110101
1010101001000
1111010101010
1010101010110
1010101011010010
1011101010010
100101010010111
100010101001100
1010001110101
1010101001000
1111010101010
1010101010110
1010101011010010
10111010101101
10111010101101
1010001110101
1010101001000
1111010101010
1010101010110
1010101011010010

Use short-term trading with no more than 20 to 30 percent of your portfolio, and no less than $5,000.

I t takes time to learn how to be a successful trader. Until you gain the necessary knowledge and experience to be a long-term day trader, the most successful strategies in the world won't help you. Therefore, we suggest that you limit the amount you use for short-term trading to only 20 to 30 percent of your portfolio. However, if that percentage comes out to less than $5,000, invest $50 or $100 every month into an index fund or mutual fund until you build up more trading capital.

Once you have the $5,000 minimum necessary to try the strategies in this book, how much is enough? If we had to summarize how much money you should start with as a long-term day trader, we would tell you to *invest only as much as you can afford to lose*. Ideally, you would have $15,000 to $20,000 to invest, because the more money you have, the more stocks you can buy. This lets you diversify among a number of securities without worrying that one losing stock will hurt you. With $5,000 or less in starting capital, you are limited to buying fewer stocks, which increases your risk and limits your profits. Remember, too, that you will need to allow funds for opening an online account to trade stocks on your own. This usually costs $2,000 to $5,000, although a couple of brokerages allow you to open an account with as little as $1,000.

Invest the remaining 70 to 80 percent of your portfolio in high quality value or growth stocks, mutual funds, or index funds. This is the key to being a long-term day trader. We admit that many of the tactics and strategies included in this book are highly aggressive and not recommended for risk-averse investors. No one should risk hard-earned money on investment strategies that make you nervous or interfere with a good night's sleep. In order to outperform the market, you must be able to adapt to changing market conditions. That is why we encourage you to use only a small portion of your portfolio to try short-term trading strategies.

After all, if you have been successful as a long-term investor, it doesn't make sense to suddenly sell all your stocks and mutual funds to try a new strategy. When you use only 30 percent of your portfolio for short-term trading, you can be aggressive without worrying that one mistake will wipe you out. We don't think you need to take unnecessary risks in order to achieve spectacular returns. The goal should be consistent returns year after year, and you can do this without jeopardizing your entire portfolio.

If, however, you are comfortable with more risk, you can make adjustments to the percentages. For example, some long-term day traders have 50 percent of their portfolios in long-term investments and use the other 50 percent for short-term trading. The final decision depends on your risk tolerance, trading capital, and financial goals.

Don't pay too much attention to the fundamentals.

Many professional money managers will tell you that the fundamentals mean everything. They spend hours studying P/E ratios, earnings reports, and lots of other ratios found on balance sheets. Based on the thousands of numbers they analyze, they will tell you whether or not they feel a company is a good investment. But there is one important factor to remember here: They are thinking long term. The recommendations they make are typically based on what they feel a stock's performance will be in the next several years. The types of trades we are teaching you will rarely last for more than a week. We do not need to own the stock for the rest of our lives. We are just renting it for a short while, then returning it once it has served our purpose. If your experience is limited to long-term investing and you have never tried short-term trading, then this may be a new concept to you. We believe the fundamentals of individual stocks do not really matter when it comes to short-term trading.

The reason for this is rather simple. You are buying and selling stocks based purely on momentum and technical market indicators. It doesn't matter whether the stock is earning a profit of $6 per share or whether it is losing $4 per share. Nor does it matter whether the P/E ratio of a stock is 20 or 200. Remember that you are not investing in the stock; you are merely using it for a few days. You are riding out momentum and playing technical factors that have been statistically proven to work over time. As your holding time decreases, so does your dependence on fundamentals. If you were going to hold the stock for the next 50 years, you would need to know everything about the company. If your holding time is one day or one week, then all you need to know is the correct stock symbol and a thorough understanding of technical analysis.

Study technical analysis.

Since you will depend significantly on technical analysis to determine which stocks you should buy or sell, you need to learn as much as you can about it. This means looking at chart patterns, volume, and price levels to help determine not only the direction of the market, but also the price direction of the stocks you want to buy. Unlike investors who are betting that the profitability of the company will continue to rise over several years, short-term day traders care more about what will happen over the next couple of days or weeks. Because you are buying and selling stocks within short time frames, *it doesn't matter if the market is up or down, as long as there is a lot of volume and price movement.*

In subsequent rules, we will describe in detail the technical indicators that will help you decide which stocks to buy. You will also learn how to recognize certain stock patterns that indicate a buying opportunity. According to most experts, you can teach almost anyone the patterns and signals to look for when deciding which stocks to buy on a short-term basis. It does, however, take additional knowledge and experience to recognize the small nuances and exceptions to the chart patterns. If you are determined to be a successful short-term trader, it is essential to learn as much as you can about technical analysis. If you combine your knowledge of technical analysis with an understanding of fundamental data about individual companies, nothing should stop you from making huge profits in the market.

Always start with practice trades.

While you are learning the techniques of short-term trading, we think it is very important to start by making practice, or make-believe, trades before you actually begin trading with your hard-earned money. Make your trades on paper or on the computer if it's easier, and track your profits or losses. Being successful at paper trades, of course, doesn't mean that you will be a great trader. When you start trading with real money, you have to deal with your emotions, primarily fear and greed. But if you can't make money on paper, that's a good indication that you might not make it as a short-term trader. Either you need to study and practice more, come up with another trading system, or stick to long-term buy-and-hold investments. Short-term trading is not for everyone, and no matter how easy it sounds in a book, it still takes skill, passion, and the ability to follow rules without exception.

Sell quickly.

When asked how long he holds his stocks, Warren Buffett once replied, "forever." Although Buffett has been wildly successful with his buy-and-hold strategy, his genius is in picking companies he can hold for a lifetime. Buffett buys stocks in companies that he knows and at prices he thinks are reasonable. This is one of the reasons he tends to avoid buying Internet stocks. If you are an investor, you could do extremely well looking for stocks that look like bargains and holding them until they reach what Buffett calls fair value.

Long-term investors will, of course, identify with Mr. Buffett. But if you are a day trader, your mission is to make a profit as quickly as possible. Obviously, if you have a long-term orientation, it isn't going to be that easy to change. The good news is that you can work yourself into it gradually with practice trades.

Generally, you will find stocks that can be played both long term and short term. Some of the technology stocks that come to mind, like Dell Computer, Ericsson, and Vitesse Semiconductor, and some of the Internet stocks, like Amazon.com and America Online, can be bought using both strategies. If you think a stock will be a superb long-term investment, buy it for the buy-and-hold portion of your portfolio.

But just because you buy a stock as a long-term investment, don't rule it out for short-term trading. Because of their volatility, a lot of these same stocks can yield great short-term profits. If you decide to buy a stock long term, chances are that you are already familiar with the company and know a lot about the fundamentals.

Study the technical indicators and make a few practice trades. For example, let's say you have a core position of 500 shares of Microsoft because you believe that it will be the dominant player in operating systems over the next 20 years. Practice trading around the position. When Microsoft looks strong, add an extra 300 shares. Conversely, if your chart indicates it looks weak, scale back to your core position. By doing so, you are able to take advantage of the short-term volatility in Microsoft.

We also successfully used this strategy with a stock called Titan Corporation (TTN). We bought 1,000 shares for the long-term portion of our portfolio. Then we made a series of short-term trades on the stock, pocketing 1- and 2-point profits as it moved up and down the chart. These are perfect examples of long-term day trading!

Select the right broker. It's more important than you think!

Several years ago, you didn't have a lot of choices with regard to types of brokers to choose from. You basically had two choices: full-service brokers or discount brokers. The full-service brokers charged higher commission rates on orders because they also provided full investment advice. The discount brokers charged lower commissions, but they did not provide any investment advice. They merely executed your orders.

Today you can choose from traditional full-service brokers, discount brokers, Web-based online brokers, and even direct-access online brokers, who offer proprietary trading software that is installed on your home computer. If you are reading this book, chances are you are not the type of person who prefers a full-service broker. Therefore, you are left with several other choices.

If you do not feel comfortable placing orders over your computer, there is nothing wrong with calling your discount broker on the phone to place orders. However, keep in mind that you will most likely be paying higher commissions for the privilege of speaking with a live human being when placing your orders. At this time, it would cost you significantly more to call in your orders to a broker than to place your orders online.

When you place an order on a Web-based broker, it is placed on your Internet browser and then e-mailed to a trader, usually at a third-party firm. The trader executes your order for you. Although this method is extremely popular, it has some significant disadvantages.

For example, most Web-based brokers sell their order flow to a market-making firm. Because the trading firm's profit is the spread between the bid and the ask price, your order will usually get filled at the highest going market price when buying, and at the lowest going market price when selling.

Another consideration with most Web-based brokers is that their systems are typically slow and not consistently reliable. Keep in mind that speed is of the essence for successful long-term day trading. If their system takes 30 seconds to accept and place your order, you will end up missing the most ideal entry and exit points for many of the trades you will be making. Also, if their system is frequently down, you will become quite frustrated.

Direct-access trading is much different than Web-based trading. It works by using independent software that is installed on your computer to place orders directly to the NASDAQ and NYSE computers. In other words, with direct-access trading, you bypass your broker's trading floor altogether. This means better order fills because your order will typically be filled by an ECN. An ECN is a network of computers that automatically matches the orders of buyers and sellers. One well-known ECN is Island (ISLD). Another benefit is that your orders will be filled much more quickly. This is important because in fast-moving markets, you will end up getting the stock at a better price if the execution is quick. However, you should know that with direct-access trading you will typically pay data and exchange fees.

Although we do not endorse any particular broker, we do recommend that you have, at the very least, a Web-based broker that uses ECNs instead of selling order flow and that has reliable networks. Even better, if you don't mind paying the extra monthly fee for data feed, is direct-access trading. Any broker that specializes in day trading will have some sort of direct-access software. In our opinion, most of the direct-access trading software is basically the same. Just make sure you choose a broker that you can count on. Saving a dollar or two on commission is not worth it if you are losing hundreds of dollars on poor fills and slow executions.

Understand the differences between the NYSE and the NASDAQ.

Although there are three primary markets, the New York Stock Exchange (NYSE), the National Association of Securities Dealers Automated Quotation System (NASDAQ), and the American Stock Exchange (AMEX), you should focus your trades on the NASDAQ and NYSE due to the large market capitalizations (caps), or high value, of the stocks that comprise them. The AMEX is typically not very good for day trading due to its lack of large market-cap stocks.

The New York Stock Exchange

The NYSE is the most highly capitalized marketplace in the world and the best known of all the exchanges. It is home to more than 3,000 companies. The market for NYSE stocks is made by one person called a specialist, with one specialist per stock. Making a market means matching buy and sell orders.

The primary reason we prefer trading NYSE stocks to NASDAQ stocks is that they tend to move in a more logical fashion. Obviously, the market as a whole has no logic to the way it moves, but NYSE stocks tend to follow more common trends than do some of the more erratic NASDAQ stocks, especially Internet stocks like Yahoo!, eBay, and CMGI. Therefore, trading based upon common indicators, such as support and resistance levels, tends to follow through with more predictable results. This is due largely to the fact that most day traders are *not* playing NYSE stocks: The stocks are able to move up and down in a more logical fashion since they are not being affected by day traders who are constantly buying and selling.

We also tend to prefer NYSE stocks because individual specialists trade them, not a group of market makers. This makes it easier for us to learn the trading style of each stock specialist.

The easiest way to identify NYSE stocks is by the number of characters in the ticker symbol. If the symbol has three or fewer characters in it, the stock is either a NYSE stock or an AMEX stock.

The NASDAQ

Founded in 1971, the NASDAQ is an electronic stock market containing more than 5,000 actively traded stocks. Most day traders prefer the NASDAQ due to the extreme volatility of some of its stocks, primarily technology and Internet stocks.

Although day traders seek volatility, we personally don't like trading the NASDAQ stocks because there are too many novice traders who trade them. This causes the stocks to reverse trends very quickly, often without just cause.

A market is made in NASDAQ stocks by a group of market makers. Depending on the market cap of the stock, there are typically anywhere from 10 to 50 market makers per stock. We see this as a disadvantage because it makes it more difficult to gauge the true buying or selling interest.

To us, it seems that the risk is higher trading NASDAQ stocks due to the extreme volatility and the multiple market makers. The NYSE stocks seem to be much easier to profitably trade, but it is a personal preference. After you have some experience under your belt, you will have to decide which exchange is right for you.

Study individual specialists and market makers.

Stocks trade as they do primarily because of their market makers' or specialists' behavior. Although an entire book could be written on dealing with market makers and specialists, let's just say that one should not to try to beat them at their own game. Many professional traders will tell you that outsmarting the market makers and specialists can be done and that you should do it, but we strongly disagree. From a logical viewpoint, how can you possibly outsmart them when you don't know what they are dealing with in terms of quantity and size of both buy and sell orders? Level II trading is helpful, but it still does not allow you to see the entire scenario. So instead of trying to outsmart them, go along with them and do as they do. For this, you must study the techniques that market makers and specialists use on the stocks you trade.

The specialists

Specialists all have different techniques for trading their stocks. Remember that there is only one specialist per stock, so it is easy to learn that person's style if you are observant. By being observant during day trading, we have learned specialists so well that we can often tell when a different specialist is trading our stocks, if, for example, the primary specialist is on vacation.

If you are able to watch stocks trade real-time during market hours, there are several points to look out for.

▸ **Does the specialist actually trade the "size" that he or she is showing?** When a NYSE or AMEX stock is quoted, there is a price and size given. The inside price represents the best bid and and the best ask. Right next to that price is a size. The size represents the number of shares available at that bid or ask. There have been countless times when a specialist showed 200,000 shares on the offer side and perhaps only 3,000 shares on the bid or buy side. When we saw that, we got scared and sold our stock, only to watch it run much higher immediately afterward. Our rationale for selling was that there were more sell orders in the specialist's book than buy orders. But we have learned not to pay much attention to the size the specialist is showing because it will often fool you. Large sizes on the offer may merely be an indication that the specialist has a large buy order coming through. Rather than simply trading the large buy order, he will often show the size first as a sell order to scare out traders. Then he immediately trades the size on the offer because he already had an order to buy that size in the first place. This may be a bit confusing, but the bottom line is simply to study the way the specialist trades size and determine the conditions and how that size is traded. Learning this will help you to know the difference between a headfake and genuine buying or selling interest.

▸ **Does the specialist exhibit any signs of an imminent movement?** Some specialists will run a stock up (move its price up) with all signs of looking normal. Others will attempt to drive the stock price down before a run-up in an attempt to shake out traders and buy their shares at a cheaper price before running it up. Still others will hold a stock at a flat price for a long time before running the stock up. The most important point to remember is that all the specialists exhibit different signs when they are going to move the stock price.

We personally have mental lists of each stock we frequently trade and how the specialist tends to move it. This has made us much better traders because if we are long in a stock that moves down quickly, we can determine whether it is a classic shakeout (a quick drop in price follwed by a quick recovery) or a real sell-off (a quick drop in price followed by more dropping). However, if we didn't pay attention and study the methods of each specialist, we would not be able to do this. Although it is impossible to list every single stock and how each tends to trade, you want to begin noticing these things and making notes of them so you are a smarter trader the next time you trade that stock.

The market makers

Unfortunately, it is harder to understand the market makers than the specialists, because there is only one specialist for every NYSE stock and there are many market makers for each NASDAQ stock. Some of the most successful traders we know prefer to stick exclusively to trading NYSE stocks for this reason.

If you do choose to trade NASDAQ stocks, we strongly recommend that you find a brokerage that offers NASDAQ Level II quotes. Level II quotes enable you to see activity on each individual market maker for any given NASDAQ stock. You can see whether a particular market maker is bidding for the stock, selling the stock, or is not really active at all in the stock. In addition, Level II allows you to see the actual quantity of market makers buying versus selling the stock. This is frequently an indication of the short-term movement of the stock. If you would like to learn more about Level II quotes, we recommend that you read *The Underground Level II Day Traders Handbook* by Jay Yu. It is available by going to *www.undergroundtrader.com.*

If you want access to Level II quotes, there is normally a monthly data and exchange fee. There are many day-trading oriented brokerage firms that offer Level II quotes. You can simply do a search on the Internet for Level II trading for more information.

Avoid trading during lunch.

The slowest period during the trading day is typically between 11:30 a.m. and 1:30 p.m. EST. There are a number of theories about why trading during these hours becomes so sluggish and is best avoided. Some believe that the senior specialists and market makers go to lunch and put their junior counterparts in charge of making the market in the stocks they are responsible for. According to this theory, the replacements are told to keep the stocks as flat as possible in order to avoid personal losses by the respective market maker or specialist. If this theory is true, the stocks don't act as they normally do because the junior market maker or specialist trades in a different style.

No matter what the reason, you must be very careful during these slow mid-day periods. It is easy to be fooled by stock movements over lunchtime because they may not truly represent the actual buying and selling interest of the stock.

The other main problem with trading during the lunch hours is liquidity. The volume usually dries up significantly during lunchtime, and this can cause larger spreads, primarily on NASDAQ stocks, and less movement. Although you will probably not get badly hurt by trading during lunch hours, getting in the habit of staying out of the market at this time will make the trading game easier, since you will be working with fewer unknowns.

Identify and avoid "pump and dump" stocks.

When we first began trading, we were intrigued by stocks that would rapidly and quite mysteriously change from relatively unknown $2 stocks to $15 "superstar" stocks that everyone in the trading world would be talking about as if they were the next Microsoft. We thought to ourselves, "Wow! 1,000-percent return! We've got to figure out how to do that!" We began looking for the next stock with the potential to explode.

In the hopes of getting rich, we invested lots of money in the next cheap stock we found that was showing strong momentum. Shortly after buying this stock, things seemed to be going well. The stock ran up fast and we were quickly in the money. "This baby is going to the moon!" was all we could think about. But then it happened. Within days of our buying the stock, it retreated back to where it started. Not only did we lose all our profit, but we were also facing a major loss. We had to find out why a seemingly unstoppable stock went from $2 to $13, and then back down to $2 within the course of one week.

After researching this particular stock on the Internet, we soon realized that we had become victims of what is commonly referred to as the "pump and dump," or P&D. A pump and dump is a scam that may be initiated by a stock promoter, a group of insiders, or a well-capitalized trader. It begins with the spread of false "inside" information or misleading valuations, disseminated through telemarketers, junk e-mail, Internet chat rooms, newsgroups, or message boards to the unsuspecting public. The goal is to create a buying frenzy—the "pump"—so they can sell their shares for a hefty profit. Once they have sold their shares, they stop their campaign, causing an avalanche of sell orders. Typically, the share price falls back to where it started. Because of the advent of the Internet, this type of fraud has become more widespread. For this reason, it is crucial that you avoid, at all costs, any stock that you suspect might be a pump-and-dump stock.

How to detect pump and dumps

Unfortunately, there is no simple, foolproof way to detect a pump and dump. Although the SEC uses tight regulation to try to prevent these things from happening, it is impossible for it to be aware of every P&D that occurs. Remember: In the world of securities trading, the Latin principle of caveat emptor—let the buyer beware—does indeed apply. Therefore, you need to learn how to identify these stocks *before* you buy them.

One piece of information you should look at when analyzing a stock is the exchange where it is listed. Many P&D schemes are orchestrated in the over-the-counter (OTC) market or the NASDAQ small-cap market. The second clue is daily volume. Was the volume steadily increasing every day over the course of several weeks (good scenario) or was the volume flat every day, suddenly spiking on a particular day (warning sign)? You should find out if there was a legitimate reason for the volume and price spike, such as great company news. If there wasn't any news associated with the runup, use extreme caution. Something is not right with this stock.

Perhaps the easiest way to avoid getting involved with a P&D stock is to simply stay away from all of the thinly traded, low-priced stocks that you never heard of before. Granted, you will occasionally miss some opportunities with runups that are indeed legitimate. But it is not worth the risk of becoming a victim of a P&D in an attempt to get rich.

By trading only stocks with large market caps (for example, IBM, Merck, General Motors, Exxon, etc.), you eliminate the risk of a P&D because these stocks are so largely traded. Our advice: Stick with these types of stocks and avoid becoming a P&D victim. Another good idea is to go to www.stockdetective.com, which educates investors on common P&D scams and how to avoid them.

Avoid rumor or tip stocks.

Has anyone ever given you a stock tip "you can't lose on"? Most likely, yes. How did the results turn out? If you are like most people, you probably put some money on the stock, had high expectations, and ended up either losing money or breaking even.

Let's face it, everyone is easily enticed by the opportunity to make a huge return with virtually no risk. It is quite difficult not to be. But, the first thing you need to realize is that the opportunity to make huge gains without risk is not possible. The larger the opportunity for high profits, the higher the risk. These two things go hand in hand.

There are a lot of people you will come across who will try to give you stock tips based on the fact that they know something about the stock that nobody else yet knows. Well, if this truly was the case, it would be considered insider trading, and we doubt that they would have told you about it in the first place. They would simply have bought the stock for themselves. The penalties for insider trading are very severe, and include the return of all profits, fines, and incarceration. Therefore, if somebody gives you a tip or a rumor on a stock, you must understand that they are probably just guessing.

The bottom line is that playing stocks based on a tip can be quite risky. Can you make money by taking someone's advice and buying the stock? Absolutely! Just be certain to *always* do your own research. You can start by researching companies at *www.sec.gov*.

Secondly, if you do buy the stock, put only a small portion of your portfolio into it. Another idea is to subscribe *to The Wall Street Journal or Investor's Business Daily*. These valuable publications will help investors or traders find stocks to buy. We recommend no more than 10 percent of your total portfolio in order to minimize the risks. If a single position can wipe out your entire account, then you are overallocated.

Hit singles, not home runs.

One of the biggest mistakes we've seen beginners make is trying to get rich quick. Another mistake is failing to cut their losses. We think that greed may be one of the reasons for these common mistakes. Greed often destroys those who would otherwise be successful traders. Remember: *Build profits one trade at a time, not with one huge trade*. Let's examine the difference.

If you are trying to gain 10 points of profit per trade, you are being greedy and will ultimately lose. On the other hand, if you are taking profits of 1 to 2 points per trade, then you are on the right track to profitability. Can you make 10 points of profit in a single trade? Sure, if you are lucky. But the operative word here is luck. Remember, the goal of the method we are teaching you is maximum profitability with minimal risk. Luck is not part of that equation; if it were, you would be gambling, and that is not what we are advocating.

Baseball fans who were around in the 1970s may remember that both Pete Rose and Mike Schmidt were successful players, but that Pete Rose was famous for hitting lots and lots of singles. Even though he didn't hit many home runs, he had a high batting average and a consistent, successful baseball career. Mike Schmidt, on the other hand, was famous for hitting lots of home runs. When he hit a home run, he scored runs and that made him successful when it happened. However, he also struck out many times while trying for home runs. Do you get the point? You can't afford to risk the many strikeouts that will inevitably happen in the process of trying for home runs. You want to be the player who hits the singles and simply gets on base in every game.

When people ask us how much profit we make on a daily basis from trading, the reactions are usually quite varied. A small percentage of people will say that they are shocked that we are able to make that much money from trading stocks. A large majority of people, however, say they are surprised that we are not making more money. The thing that most people don't understand is that we don't try to make more than we do because we know that greed will take over if we try for too much profit. We have found that we are much more successful by simply aiming for *consistent daily profits.* Remember, *it's not about the money that you earn, it's all about the money that you don't lose.* It's the losses that hurt most traders. The way to wealth in trading is through building consistent daily profits. Hit singles, not home runs.

Learn how to sell short.

To be a successful short-term trader, we believe it is absolutely essential to learn how to trade during all market conditions, and that includes short selling. Instead of investing in a stock and betting that it will go up, traders who short a stock are betting that the stock will go down. Short selling can be hard for long-term investors to understand, because it runs contrary to their usual approach. For this reason, our discussion of this rule will be more comprehensive than some of the others we present in this book.

Since we have been in a bull market for the past so many years, most people who trade stocks are used to simply buying a stock, holding on to it, waiting for the price to go up, and selling it. This is known as going long or being long a stock. Obviously, the profit then becomes the difference between the price the investor paid for the stock and the price that the stock was sold for. This is by far the most common method of trading a stock.

Going long in a bull market is quite profitable, but we firmly believe that this great bull market we are in will eventually end or at least slow down. Obviously, nobody knows exactly when this will happen. It could be tomorrow, it could be next year, or it could be 15 years from now. But eventually, we will have a bear market. And even if it does take 15 years for a bear market to come, there will still be many periods of correction in the market along the way. Corrections are merely short-term downtrends that occur during a bull market. When we are in either a bear market or a temporary correction period, it becomes very difficult to make short-term profits by going long on stocks. Obviously, this challenges primarily short-term traders, not typical investors whose time frames for holding a stock are much longer. However, the great news is that you can make just as much of a profit in a down market as you can in an up market if you learn to master short selling.

What is short selling?

Short selling is very similar to going long a stock, except that the order of the buying and selling process is reversed. Instead of buying a stock and then selling it, you sell the stock first, then buy it back at a later time. To do this, you borrow shares of a stock from your broker—shares you do not actually own—and then sell them with the expectation that the price of the stock will drop. The reason you want the price to drop is because you must eventually buy the stock back to replace the stock that you borrowed. Your profit or loss then becomes the difference between the price at which you sold the stock and the price at which you bought the stock back. If the price of the stock drops, you make a profit. If the price increases, you will incur a loss. The process of borrowing the shares and then immediately selling them is known as selling short. The process of buying back the shares that you borrowed is known as covering your short position.

Let's look at an example. Suppose you think that the price of International Paper (IP) is going to decline over the next couple of weeks, so you decide to go short the stock. You place the order to sell short 500 shares at a price of 64 1/8. Your order gets filled, and you are now short 500 shares of IP. This means that, instead of owning 500 shares of IP, you owe 500 shares that you borrowed from your broker. Let's assume that, two weeks later, the price of the stock drops to 61. You decide that the stock will probably not drop much lower, so now is the best time to buy back your borrowed shares because you want to buy your shares back at the lowest possible price. You place your order to buy 500 shares of IP at a price of 61, and your order gets filled. You have now just covered your short position with a profit of 3 1/8 points per share. This is because you sold the stock at a price of 64 1/8 and bought the stock back at a price of 61. Your profit is the difference between the price at which you sold the stock and the price at which you bought it back. In this case, that equates to a profit of 3 1/8 points per share.

Short selling is in many ways very similar to going long, but the order of the process is reversed. In both cases, your profit is the difference between the price you paid when you bought the stock and the price you paid when you sold it. The primary difference is that the selling occurs before the buying when you are short. If you are long, then you first must buy the stock, then sell it. If you are buying a stock long, the goal is to buy as low as possible and subsequently sell as high as possible. When you are short a stock, the goal is to sell short at as high a price as possible and subsequently buy the stock back, or cover, at as low a price as possible. Both situations will yield the maximum profit for you.

The benefits of shorting stocks

The most obvious benefit of shorting stocks is that it enables you to make a profit in a down market. Being able to make money in a down market is crucial to your success if you intend to make a career at trading stocks. But, just as important, shorting enables you to make money on stocks that are going down, even in the midst of a bull market, by taking advantage of corrections and sell-offs in the market. By shorting stocks in addition to going long, you are giving yourself twice as many opportunities to profit because you are taking advantage of both upward and downward momentum in the market.

Every superstar stock that runs up eventually comes down. It may come down and then quickly resume the upward trend, but it will always pull back at least to some degree before going higher. If you master shorting, you can learn to take advantage of these pull-backs and sell-offs by shorting these stocks before they drop.

One of the best parts about shorting stocks is that downward momentum in a stock is often much more rapid than upward momentum. This is because stocks that are going up are constantly seeing profit taking along the way, which often causes the upward movement to slow. However, when the stocks are coming down, they are usually met with panic selling along the way, which causes the decline to be even more severe. Therefore, the percentage of profit to be made by shorting can often be higher than going long.

The risks of shorting stocks

Although shorting stocks can be quite profitable, it is imperative that you understand the risks of short selling, which can be very high if not kept under control. The greatest risk in short selling is the fact that, unlike with going long, you can lose an unlimited amount of money if you do not cut your losses.

When you buy a stock, the maximum amount of money that you can lose is limited to the initial amount of money that you invest. For example, if you buy 100 shares of a stock at 35, the maximum amount of money you can lose is the initial amount of money you invested, in this case $3,500. Your maximum loss is $3,500 because the price of the stock cannot go any lower than zero. However, when you sell short a stock, the losses can be much greater, even infinite.

Let's suppose that you sell short a stock at 48, and then the stock starts to rise in price. Instead of cutting your losses, you wait longer, hoping that the stock will come back down to a lower price. You watch in horror and amazement as the price of that stock goes to 100, 200, 300, or more! At some point, you are going to be forced to cover your position. Finally, sick to your stomach, you cover your position at a price of 200. You have just lost 152 points on that stock! So you see, you can actually lose more money than what you paid for the stock. Therefore, you must keep your losses under control and cut them quickly.

When you are investing for the long term and buy a stock that drops in price, you can wait for the price of the stock to come back to where you bought it if you don't want to take a big loss. However, when you short stocks, the price may very well never drop back to the price you sold short at. As such, it is crucial that you cut losses quickly when shorting stocks. We can't stress that point enough. Don't let a small loss turn into a major heartache for you.

The short-selling mentality

When we first began shorting stocks, it took us quite a while until we became comfortable with the whole concept of it. After all, it seemed odd to be excited when stock prices dropped or the market was selling off. But we soon learned that this was just part of the fun of shorting.

When we tell other traders that we frequently short stocks, they often tell us that shorting is un-American and that we are pessimists because we are shorting instead of going long. We think they must not understand the whole concept of shorting. The simple fact of the matter is that we want to profit in the market by going both ways. We see no logical reason to limit our trades to only going long. It just doesn't make sense to us. You need to realize that most investors you meet are not nearly as sophisticated as professional traders, and as such they do not understand the many benefits of shorting. It is not un-American, pessimistic, or anything else. It is simply a way to make money!

The successful short seller also knows that it is not wise to short a stock simply because you feel it is overvalued and priced too high. That type of thinking will absolutely kill you. A friend of ours once shorted Qualcomm (QCOM) when it was trading around $65 per share because he felt the stock was way overvalued and that it should be trading at a much lower price. "That company should be trading at about a quarter of what it is," he would tell us. Unfortunately, other traders and investors did not feel the same. At the time of this writing, Qualcomm was trading at around $670 per share. Instead of cutting his loss quickly, he just watched the stock price go up every day until he finally decided to cover his position with an almost 60-point loss. He was fortunate that he covered at around $125, because he would have been looking at a loss of more than $600 per share.

The moral of the story? Shorting a stock just because you think it is overvalued is not wise. Although it might really be overvalued, it doesn't matter. As long as other traders and investors continue buying the stock, its price will continue to rise. Fundamentals don't matter in this situation. Shorting a stock just because you feel it is overvalued is like stepping in front of a freight train because you think it has enough time to stop.

The mechanics of shorting

One of the most overlooked, but most important, mechanics of shorting is the uptick rule. This is a rule, imposed by the SEC, that prevents you from short selling a stock as it drops in price. It requires you to wait for some buyers to come into the stock. This rule was imposed to prevent short sellers from killing the price of a stock that is already on the way down.

The uptick rule basically means that you are only allowed to short a stock if the price at which it is trading is increasing. For example, if a stock trades at 40 11/16 after trading at 40 5/8, there has been uptick, or increase, in the price. Therefore, you would be able to go short the stock at a price of 40 11/16 or higher. However, if the stock trades 40 5/8, then trades 40 1/2, then 40 3/8, then 40 5/16, you will not be able to get your short sale order filled until the stock turns around and upticks to a price that is higher than the previous trade. This often makes it somewhat difficult to get your short sale orders filled. Therefore, the key is getting the short sale order filled before the stock starts to drop in price.

It is also important to realize that you may be at an immediate loss as soon as your short order gets filled. That is because for the order to get filled, the stock must uptick to your price that you have set. Typically, the price of the stock will continue to go even higher. However, this should not be a concern if you shorted the proper stock at the proper time, because you know the price will soon drop back down to a price that is lower than the price that you shorted at. It just requires a great deal of patience.

Speaking of which, patience is very important when shorting. It will sometimes take a while before a stock drops, but when it does, it will usually be quick and dramatic. Remember that the stock will be against you immediately after your short order gets filled. You cannot be scared into covering the stock as soon as you are filled. As long as you select the proper sector or stocks for shorting, sit tight and wait, giving the stock some room to run a little more to the upside. We learned that from experience.

In the late summer of 1999, after doing a great deal of technical analysis, we shorted Hewlett Packard (HWP) at a price of 90 3/4. After shorting the stock, we waited and waited for it to drop, but nothing happened. Two hours later, it had moved up to 91 1/8, which was not really that much of a loss for us, but we got bored waiting for the stock to drop. As a result, we covered it at a price of 91. What happened next we will never forget. No more than 30 minutes later, HWP totally crumbled and fell apart. We're not talking a 1/2 point, 1 point, or even 2 points. The stock dropped almost 5 points to a price of just over 86! If we had had just a little more patience, and waited a little longer, we would have made a several-point profit. Patience is crucial when shorting.

We also recommend that you take your profits quickly when shorting. This means that if the stock drops 2 points, take your profit. Don't wait for it to drop another 2 points, because you risk the possibility that it will suddenly rally, in which case you would lose your profit. Stocks that are dropping tend to reverse course quickly when new buyers come in. This is due only in part to the new buyers coming in. The rest of the sudden reversal occurs when those people that are short are suddenly forced to cover, thus causing even more buying to happen in the stock, and causing the price to rise even quicker. This is commonly referred to as a short squeeze. Since you don't want to be caught in one of those, the best way to avoid it is to take profits quickly.

Although most traders only go long, you will be able to make a much more consistent profit if you can learn to take advantage of shorting. In fact, the most consistently profitable traders we know are the ones who short stocks as frequently as they go long.

Remember that the three most important factors in successful shorting are patience, applying strict discipline with regard to stop losses, and taking profits quickly. If you can consistently remember these three factors, select the proper sectors and stocks for shorting, and ignore what the masses say about shorting, you will quickly become a very profitable and consistent short-term trader.

Never average down a loss.

If you are an experienced investor and are new to short-term trading, then this concept will go against everything you have been taught.

Investors are often taught to always average down good quality stocks that are temporarily not doing well for them. This means that if you originally bought General Motors (GM) at a price of $68, but then it dropped to $61 a month later, you would be encouraged to buy more shares at the price of $61. The benefit of this is that your average buying price now becomes lower than the original $68 you paid. Therefore, it becomes easier and quicker to make a profit once the stock rises again. It is important to understand that the whole reason the concept of averaging down works in long-term investing is because you are basing your decisions on the fact that you are investing in quality companies that are almost certain to bounce back to a higher price eventually.

Short-term trading, on the other hand, is an entirely different concept. You are merely looking for a quick profit, based upon a variety of technical analyses. Therefore, you do not want to average down a losing short-term trade because you just may end up with a stock that never comes back to the price you bought it at. Instead of a loss from just buying the initial shares, you are now looking at a major loss because you bought the stock twice. Now it is even lower than both of your buy prices. The bottom line for long-term day traders is that most of the time when you average down a losing position, the loss just ends up becoming larger.

Another major problem with averaging down is that you end up tying up your excess buying power, which prevents you from being able to trade other stocks that would eventually end up being more profitable for you. So, instead of making up for your loss by making several new trades, you end up waiting for your stocks to come back to a break-even point or better so that you can close your positions. It is always better to just take the loss, move on, and make a new trade. You will be amazed at how much quicker you will recoup your losses by placing some new trades.

Limit your losses; get out quickly if a stock goes against you.

One of the hardest decisions anyone has to make in the market is whether to hold a stock for additional profits or sell to lock in gains. If we could tell you exactly when to sell a stock, we would never have to work again! Even the experts don't agree on the best time to sell individual stocks. For every rule, there are dozens of exceptions.

Nevertheless, we can give you some general guidelines. Some short-term traders recommend you sell when you achieve a 30 or 35 percent profit. If you don't sell everything, they say, then at the very least sell half of your shares. Others recommend that you slowly unload your position as the stock price rises. By the time the stock has reached its high, you will have sold off all your shares. The advantage of this strategy is that you won't be left with a huge position if the stock turns against you. Still other traders go by instinct, especially short-term traders who seem to know when the volume is drying up and the price levels are retreating. This is instinct based on knowledge.

All trading pros, however, recommend that you use stop losses to lock in your gains. To our way of thinking, the single most fatal mistake a short-term trader can make is failing to limit losses. In fact, if you don't plan to follow this rule, none of the other rules really matter. We don't mean to sound threatening, but we have personally seen the downfall of many traders who would have been successful if they had followed this simple rule.

Why do so many traders fail to cut their losses? After all, it is not a technically difficult thing to do: All you need to do is place a sell order. But psychologically, cutting losses on a stock goes against the basic principles of investing that have been ingrained into our heads since we first started trading.

Investors generally do not worry much about cutting losses. Because the time horizon of an investor is typically at least five years or more, they feel they have time to wait for the stock to come back up to the price at which they bought it. Investors have learned that, even though the market will have many ups and downs in the short term, quality stocks will always come back up over the long term. Therefore, an investor would have no logical reason to cut losses on a quality stock that goes against them.

As a short-term trader, though, you must realize that totally different rules apply. Your time horizon is usually several days to a week, not several years. You cannot afford to be stuck holding a stock with a large loss. Although there are quite a few reasons that cutting losses on stocks is crucial to traders, here are the two that are most important:

Short-term traders cannot afford to have their capital tied up.

Because a short-term trader makes profits by making many trades during the course of several days or weeks, it is important that cash equity always be available to enter into trades at the right moment. If, on the other hand, all your equity is in the form of stocks that have large losses, you will not be able to enter into any new positions that can potentially become profitable. We are speaking from experience when we say that it is very frustrating not to have any cash to buy a skyrocketing stock because you are sitting with a bunch of losing positions that you should have dumped a long time ago. So, even though you are losing a small amount of money each time you cut losses on a losing position, it is a lot worse when you cannot buy a new stock because you don't have enough money.

Many of the stocks that short-term traders buy may *not* come back to the price they bought them at.

It is important to remember that a short-term trader enters into positions for totally different reasons than an investor. An investor will buy a stock because he feels the stock will rise in price over the long term due to the fundamentals of a particular company. This means that investors buy stocks based upon factors such as earnings, growth rate, etc. Investors are confident that the stocks they buy will eventually keep setting new highs because the companies they buy are fundamentally strong companies that will continue to grow.

Instead, a short-term trader buys a stock because he feels the stock will move in the right direction over the short term based upon technical factors, not the company's fundamentals. This means that a short-term trader expects the stock to move in the right direction in the short term due to technical reasons, but this does not mean that the stock will perform at all in the long term. Some of the stocks that we trade are stocks that we would never consider buying as investors. Therefore, if a stock doesn't move the way you expect it to, get out quickly because it may never rise back up to the price you bought it at.

Although buying based on statistically proven technical methods will be effective a majority of the time, it won't be all of the time. Therefore, you need to realize when you made a bad decision, cut the losses quickly, and get out. No excuses!

When we are short-term trading, we have a tendency to look back on the stocks that we cut our losses on to see whether or not the stock went further down or bounced back up once we sold it.

Every once in a while, a stock that we cut our losses on will sky-rocket up immediately after we sell it. This is very frustrating, in-deed, and seeing it happen sometimes tempts us to break the rule of cutting our losses. However, a majority of the time, the stock con-tinues to fall further once we sell it, and often never bounces back up to the price we sold at. These are the trades that remind us why it is crucial to cut losses quickly. Remember that we cannot win at every single trade, but we can put the odds of profitability in our favor.

Types of stop losses

There are basically two types of stop losses that you can use. There are mental stops and physical stops. Understanding the differ-ence between the two and knowing which is best for you is very important.

If you use a mental stop loss, that simply means that you de-cide in your head that you will sell your position once the stock trades up to or down to a certain price. Mental stop losses need to be decided upon before ever entering the actual position. In other words, there must be a predetermined exit strategy even before get-ting into the position. Then, if that stock does indeed hit that price, you need to have the discipline to stick to your mental stop and quickly cut your loss.

The benefit of using a mental stop, as opposed to a physical stop loss, is that the specialists and market makers will not know that you are using a stop loss, and you therefore have less of a chance of getting unjustifiably taken out of a position.

Mental stops are typically the best kind of stops to use be-cause they allow you to get better fills and also get shaken out of stocks less often. However, be aware that they also only work if you have the discipline to stick to the mental stops that you set in your head. If you know that you do not have the proper discipline necessary to stick to your mental stops, then you will be better off using a physical stop loss order. Mental stops require great discipline.

Besides demanding discipline, mental stops require you to physically watch the market and your stock at all times during the trading day. You need to watch it so that you will be aware if the stock trades at the price that will cause you to cut your loss. If you can't track the prices of your positions throughout the day, then using a mental stop will not work for you.

Placing a physical stop loss order means that you place an order with your broker that will cause your broker to automatically place a sell order in the event that a stock trades down to a specified price. There are two types of physical stop loss orders: "stop limit" orders and "stop market" orders.

A stop limit order means that once the stock trades down to or up to the price you specify, a limit order will then be placed for you to sell the stock at your specified price or better. The benefit of using a limit order is that you will get a better price for your sell order. However, the major disadvantage is that your order may never become executed at all. This is because your order will only be filled if your limit price is hit. In a quickly declining stock, it is entirely possible, and probable, that a stock will drop below your stop limit order, keep on going lower, and never even execute your order. Therefore, we recommend that you always use stop market orders instead. They are much more reliable because once the stock reaches the price you specify, your sell or buy order then becomes a market order, meaning that your order will be executed at whatever the next price is. You may end up losing a little bit more than what you plan on, but at least you will be out of the stock. Why worry about losing 1/8 or so for the risk that you may lose several points if your stop limit order doesn't get filled?

Let's look at a few examples to explain the difference. Assume you are long Sears at a price of 47 3/4, and the stock is currently trading at 48. You decided when you first entered the position that you want to sell your stock and cut your loss if it trades down to a price of 46 1/2. You therefore place a stop market order at a price of 46 1/2. The next morning, unbeknownst to you, Sears announces some bad news before the opening bell. They open at 47, but quickly drop down to 46 1/2. As soon as the stock trades, your stop market order now goes live and you now have an order out there to sell your shares at the market price. The stock drops lower, and you get filled at 46 1/4. But, at least you are out. On the other hand, if you had placed a stop limit order at 46 1/2, there is a very good possibility that your order would not have gotten executed at all, depending on how fast the stock was dropping. The stock likely would have dropped quickly past the 46 1/2, thereby leaving your stop limit sell order untouched. Next thing you know, you are looking at a several-point loss because you didn't use a stop market order.

Now that you understand the options that you have with regard to placing stop orders, you need to know at what point to cut your losses. Unfortunately, there is no clear cut answer as to exactly what value to use for a stop loss. Several factors will affect the value you use. For one thing, it is largely a personal decision, based primarily upon your risk tolerance. You may feel more comfortable with a larger stop loss, while the trader down the road from you wants to use a tighter stop loss. Either way is okay, but just make sure that you use one.

It is also important to understand that the size of your stop loss needs to vary based on both the price and volatility of the individual stocks you are trading. A volatile stock such as Amazon.com (AMZN) can and will easily move up or down 2 or 3 points within several minutes. Therefore, a stop loss of only 1 point would be virtually useless. However, if you use a 1-point stop loss on a stock like Disney, that would be fine because Disney is a much less volatile stock. As a rule, the more volatile the stock is, the more "wiggle room" you need to give it.

The price of a stock will also determine how much wiggle room you need to allow. A stock that is trading at $380 is going to move up or down many more points than a similar stock that is trading at $20. However, keep in mind that a 10-point move on a $100 stock is exactly the same percentage gain or loss as a 1-point move on a $10 stock. Keep that in mind when setting your stop losses, too.

In summary, cutting your losses on a stock is mentally one of the most challenging things to do. Admitting your mistakes and moving on quickly to the next opportunity is a key to success. Even more important is to learn from all your losses. It takes every ounce of courage for us to sell one of our stocks at a loss. Trust us when we tell you that you will save yourself a lot of money, heartache, and pain over the long run if you follow this one simple rule.

Don't trade unless you're mentally prepared.

There have been many days in our careers when we sat down in front of our computers, turned on our data feeds, and were physically ready to trade. But for some reason, we just weren't able to get our thoughts together; we were totally distracted. This typically occurred when we had some sort of emotional situation happening in our lives, such as a pending decision that was weighing on us or a disagreement with a family member, or even when we were just physically tired. When this occurs, it is very dangerous to trade because you are not as focused as you should be. Without focus, you might as well forget about trying to make a profit.

We've also had times when we would have uneasy feelings about trading on a particular day that could not always be logically explained. It didn't matter to us. If we didn't feel right about trading, we knew it would be a wasted day. Although you may well miss out on some opportunities by not trading on such days, you will be much better off. Missed money is always better than lost money. Remember that staying out of the market may be one of the best trades that you ever made. Never be afraid to sit on the sidelines if you are not mentally prepared—whatever the reason.

Don't trade scared.

What exactly does it mean to trade scared? There was once a commercial for an online brokerage that showed a man trying to get up enough nerve to push the buy button on his computer. Scary music played in the background. Although this example is a bit extreme, there are indeed traders that we know who act exactly like the man in the commercial. Scared traders are trading with money they need for basic essentials or who lack self-confidence. If you are not prepared mentally, you cannot be successful.

These are traders who will study stocks during the entire course of the day, talk about great stocks to trade, but yet lack the confidence or courage to execute the trades themselves. The sad part is that many of these people actually have the knowledge to be profitable traders and have the ability to see potentially profitable trades. They just lack the confidence to quickly execute their plan. This is not the way to trade because it is virtually impossible to be a profitable trader if you are questioning your own ability or are incapacitated by fear.

There are several factors that cause people to trade scared. The biggest one is trading with scared money. Scared money is money that you cannot afford to lose. This could include trading with your life savings, retirement money, money borrowed from a friend or relative, or money that needs to be used to pay your monthly expenses. If you are trading under any of these conditions, stop right now! We can assure you that you will not be at your peak comfort level, and as a result, your performance as a trader will suffer. It takes a clear head to be a successful trader and it is impossible to have a clear head if you are playing with money that is too precious to lose. If this is the only money you have to trade with, you probably should not be practicing short-term day trading at all.

Remember that knowing day-trading techniques does not necessarily mean being able to make trades. If practice trading has not given you the confidence you need and you are still fearful of making trades, perhaps you should stick with the buy-and-hold strategies of long-term investing.

Be patient.

In an earlier rule, we explained how important it is to be patient when you are shorting. Patience is such a critical requirement of short-term trading, however, that we feel it deserves a rule of its own.

At first thought, a patient day trader may seem to be another oxymoron. After all, how can anyone who is constantly buying and selling stocks, sometimes within a matter of minutes, be considered a patient person? We realize the whole concept may seem a little contradictory, but patience really is crucial as a short-term trader. Patience applies to two main scenarios in trading. The first scenario is having patience to stay in a stock the proper amount of time in order for the trade to be profitable. The second is having faith in your indicators and patience to let them work.

First and foremost, patience is crucial when choosing any new position. The technical analysis tactics you will be learning in this book have produced very accurate results—statistically speaking—with regard to making a profit in short time frames. However, no amount of technical analysis will ever tell you exactly when a certain move in a given stock will happen. We can estimate it, but we can never know exactly. Therefore, you need to have the patience to allow the methods to work.

We have countless examples and reminders of our impatience, where, if we had waited just a few hours longer, a trade would have worked out great. But we got impatient and sold at break-even. Perhaps we second-guessed ourselves or lost faith in our technical indicators. Whatever the reason, we simply needed to have more patience with the stock and more patience with our data.

You also need to be patient with yourself while you are learning. Although it is simple for some people to learn technical analysis and memorize the proper things to do, the act of trading with real money in a real market can be much more difficult because of emotions. Even when you eventually learn all the rules of how to trade, the variances in the market and the different situations you encounter will often prove frustrating for you. So be patient with yourself. Most professional traders agree that you need to give yourself at least six months to one year to start to become a decent trader.

Trade like a robot, without emotion.

Let's pretend that you just made a trade in Wal-Mart and it turned out to be a losing trade. You did everything right in making the trade, but you still ended up having to use your stop loss. So, now you've lost 1 point on 1,000 shares and you are pretty mad at the stock. "This stock will not outdo me," you say to yourself. So, you again make another trade in Wal-Mart, except that this time you don't even do any analysis. You simply buy it back out of anger at your loss. But, again you are forced to take a loss in the trade. Getting more and more frustrated, you enter the trade once again like a madman, totally out of control, and acting purely on emotion and without logic until you are in a vicious downward spiral.

If you have traded stocks for any length of time, there is a good possibility that this has happened to you. The preceding scenario is commonly referred to as vengeance trading. As you can imagine, it is a very unprofitable way of trading, and it can in fact lead to great losses. It is only human to get upset when you make a bad trade or the stock doesn't do what you want it to. But, the worst possible thing you can do is try to win your money back. Remember one very important thing...stocks are inanimate objects without any emotions. They simply react to the buying and selling interest of the public. When you really think about it, it is ridiculous to try to get back at a stock.

The most successful traders we know are those who trade like robots. Instead of acting on emotion, they merely do what their technical training has taught them to do. If the indicators say to buy, they buy, and vice versa. They do not try to change the market, they merely react to it. Remember that no amount of emotion on your part is going to change the outcome of the market. So, it is crucial that you trade stocks based purely on logic. Don't second guess yourself. Just do what your technical training has taught you to do and keep emotion out of the picture.

Always have a profit goal.

When we first began our careers as traders, we really didn't have much direction or focus with regard to how much profit we were trying to make on a daily or a weekly basis. Instead, we just went through the motions and would simply try to make as much money as we could. Unfortunately, this is not a very productive way to trade because it does not give you a goal.

It really doesn't matter what type of goal you set for yourself or whether it's a daily, weekly, or monthly goal. The important point is that you make sure that you have one. Some people set monetary goals, while others set goals for a specific number of points of profit. Personally, we prefer to have a goal to earn a specific number of points per week. If we buy a stock at 50 and sell it at 52, then we made a profit of 2 points. But, if we do that with four different stocks during the course of one week, that would give us a total profit of 8 points.

Our personal goal is to make a profit of about 8 points per week consistently. A point is equivalent to $1. To calculate your monetary profits, you would simply multiply the number of points of profit times the number of shares you are trading with during each trade. If you trade 1,000 shares at a time, that would equal about $8,000 per week. If you only trade 300 shares at a time, then that would equal about $2,400 per week.

When setting a financial goal for trading, be sure that the goal is one that motivates you, but at the same time is realistic enough to achieve. As short-term traders, we set goals on a daily basis, but weekly goals may make more sense depending on the period of time over which you are trading. What is a realistic profit goal? An average weekly profit of 5 points is both realistic and quite doable, but an average weekly profit of 20 points is not realistic. It will happen every once in a while, but it is not likely that it will happen on a consistent basis.

What we have found is that we are able to average about a 200 percent to 300 percent annual return by short-term trading. Therefore, for us, it is not realistic to earn 1,000 percent return per year. If you begin trading with an account equity of $20,000, for example, it would not be very realistic to say that you want to make $1,000 per day. That doesn't mean that you won't occasionally have a $1,000 day. But it is highly unlikely that you would be able to maintain a consistent $1,000 per day if you are only trading with $20,000 in equity. That would be the equivalent of $264,000 per year in profits, which is roughly equal to a 1,300 percent return. Let us just say that we would be highly impressed if that were to happen. A more realistic goal is 100 to 300 percent annual returns, and that is after you have become very good at trading.

To help you figure out a weekly goal, let's assume that you have $50,000 in equity to trade with and start off with a goal of 100 percent return per year. If that is the case, you would then divide $50,000 by 52 weeks per year, which is approximately $961 per week. You could say then that your weekly profit goal is $961 per week.

The main thing to keep in mind is that it really doesn't matter whether your goal is 50 percent, 100 percent, 200 percent, or 300 percent per year, as long as you have one. Having an actual monetary goal has three main benefits. First, it allows you to feel very satisfied when you obtain your goal on a consistent basis. You can be less stressed when making trades. Second, it prevents greed from creeping into the picture because you won't worry about making more money once you make your weekly goal. In fact, we usually stop trading once we have achieved our daily profit goals. Third, it gives you some kind of feedback on your performance. Without having a goal, you have no real way of measuring your success, and, more importantly, your personal improvements over time.

Always keep a personal trading log.

The longer we are in this business, the more amazed we become by traders who do not keep trading logs. We can't really blame them because we also never kept any when we first started trading. However, one thing we can tell you for certain is that our results improved dramatically when we started keeping logs.

Why is a trading log important? After all, you are indeed aware of what is happening as the trading day transpires. Why put forth the extra effort to write it all down? Primarily, it is an exercise in self-analysis so that you can improve and continue growing as a trader.

When you begin short-term trading, you will quickly realize that you will make many mistakes. That is to be expected, because you can't possibly make a profit without making a fair number of mistakes. However, if you are not physically writing down each mistake you make, you are bound to repeat the same mistakes many more times, most likely the next day.

Before we began keeping a trading log, it seemed as if the mistakes we made were recurring at least once a week. This happened because we didn't have a written record of the mistakes in front of us. But once we started keeping and reviewing a trading log, we soon discovered that our mistakes began to cease because our trading logs were constantly reminding us of them.

The log also plays a crucial role in showing you what conditions exist when you do something right. You are more likely to do the correct thing if you are constantly being reminded about what you do well.

As you can see, the reasons for keeping a log are plentiful. But what exactly do you need to keep in your log? Here is what we keep track of:

> ▸ **Notes on the movement and behavior of individual stocks.** As we previously mentioned in this book, it is crucial to keep track of your observations. By keeping

track of what you observe about each stock, you will be much more efficient and profitable the next time you trade that stock. For example, in our log, we have notations about which stocks always try to shake us out of them right before a big runup in price. If we didn't make note of this, we would easily forget which stocks tend to do this to us. In addition, we also make note of any special characteristics that stocks exhibit before they make big moves in either direction. By keeping track of this, we know what signs to look for the next time we are trading that stock. It really doesn't matter exactly which details you write about each stock; just make sure that you write down any specific observations because those situations will indeed occur again.

▶ **Notes on personal weaknesses.** This is similar to making note of the mistakes you tend to make. In this section of our logs, we write down all the dumb things we do that cause us to make bad trades that should otherwise have been profitable. Obviously, this list is going to be different for everyone, but just be sure to be honest with yourself when writing your list. The log is strictly for your benefit, so being dishonest will only end up hurting you. If you do not force yourself to recognize and admit your weaknesses, you will never improve as a trader. Accepting the mistakes you make and, more importantly, writing them down to prevent them from happening again is crucial to your long-term success as a trader.

▶ **Notes on what you do well.** You will find that there are certain factors that tend to happen whenever you make a profitable trade. These are the things that you do well and the good habits that you want to make sure you keep and try to do more often. Again, the list will be highly dependent on your own personality, but just make sure that you make a list.

▸ **A list of the 10 most important personal trading rules.**
This is where you list your 10 most important trading
rules, either taken from this book or others, or from your
personal trading experience. When you have finished com-
piling the rules, print them out and post them on your
monitor. They will help keep you on track.

Once you have gathered this large collection of rules, notes, and
comments for the benefit of self-analysis, it is crucial that you do the
next step, the most important one: Review your log every day. What
good is it if you never look at it? Each day before the market opens,
spend just 10 minutes or so reviewing your notes. If you are religious
about keeping a log, you will be amazed at how much this begins to
help your trading performance.

Realize that losses are going to happen and accept it.

Let's face it. Trading stocks can be quite frustrating and emotional. There will be some weeks when you are raking in the dough,
riding high, feeling like you are an unstoppable superhuman trading
machine. And there will also be many weeks when you wonder why
you ever decided to place a stock trade to begin with. We have never
met a trader who did not want to quit trading at some point in his or
her career. If people ever tell you otherwise, you can be sure they are
fooling themselves. It is important that you realize that even professional traders get stuck in ruts and have losing periods. The difference is in how they react to the losses.

When someone asks a professional trader how he or she did for
the day, the professional trader responds with "great," no matter
what the results really were. Even if it was a losing day, the true
professional still understands that a lot was learned, and that therefore it was a good day. A person will never know if the professional trader had a profitable or losing day because the attitude is
the same either way.

Like the pros, successful short-term traders should view losing weeks as an opportunity to examine their techniques and see how they can improve. You can analyze each trade and figure out what you could have done differently. The professionals know that mistakes often teach us the best lessons.

Unsuccessful short-term traders, on the other hand, get very discouraged by losing weeks. They let their results impact their attitude, which starts them on a vicious downward cycle. The negativity clouds their thinking, they lose their ability to reason future trades, and, most important, they lose hope. They stop following the rules, they don't cut their losses, and they whine about their losing stocks. Instead of analyzing their trades and learning from their mistakes, they simply make excuses for poor trades and point the finger at something or someone else. Losing traders may be able to identify their mistakes, yet they continue to make the same mistakes time and again. The losing trader also complains when someone asks how he or she did for the day.

Losing is part of the game; view it like a business. A business will have profitable times and losing times. No business will ever go without the occasional loss. A successful businessperson knows the key to success is simply to have more profitable times than losing times. The same principle applies to trading. Accept that you will have losing trades. As long as you win more than you lose, guess what the end result will be? Profit. If you were profitable in your trading before and you suddenly start losing, don't forget that you really do have the ability to succeed at trading: You just got temporarily sidetracked. So go back and study your personal trading log. Analyze what you did right during the profitable times and see if you are still doing those things. Most likely, you will discover that the only thing preventing you from changing your results is your attitude.

Finally, make sure you never let the word "hope" enter into your trading vocabulary. You never want to find yourself in a trade saying, "I hope the stock comes back soon." When you enter a trade, it is based on your analysis of the market. If you are still in a trade based on hope, it really means you are not willing to accept that you were wrong. All the hope in the world will not make a stock reverse its course, so don't make the mistake of holding on to it. When you are wrong, accept it and simply cut your losses as quickly and cleanly as possible. Keep hope out of the picture and you'll be a more profitable trader.

Have a strategy for dealing with losses.

Although you may have lofty profit goals and you are ready to accept the fact that you will lose from time to time, how will you deal with those losing days? While losers simply complain about their losses, the professional trader has a strategy for dealing with them.

One of the biggest mistakes we've seen people make when having a losing period is to double up on their average share size in an attempt to try to "win back their losses." When people are down on their losses, they tend to get emotional and start revenge trading. Actually, the proper thing to do is exactly the opposite. Instead of "doubling up," they need to scale back their average share size. This helps to preserve capital in the event that the losing streak continues. Once things begin to turn around, then gradually they can return to their normal share size.

Mentally, the best thing we have found to help us get out of losing streaks is to string together our winning trades, no matter how minimal the profits. This means that we try to get as many consecutive wins in a row, with no losses at all. When trying to string together our winning trades, we are not concerned about the dollar amount of profit we make. Instead, we simply make it our goal to make as many profitable trades in a row as possible, no matter how minimal the profits may be. By doing this, we quickly rebuild our confidence in our ability to trade. We would much rather go home with a profit of only $50 for the day than go home with a loss. It is amazing how therapeutic it is to have a bunch of consecutive profitable days, even if the profits are minimal.

Practice cherry picking.

In our earlier years, when our trading capital was much more limited, we were overly cautious about avoiding even the smallest loss because we couldn't afford to lose; our accounts were too small to handle losses. The problem with this, as we tell you repeatedly, is that you will have losses. If your account is not large enough to handle even small losses, or if you do not have a strategy for dealing with your losses, then you will not have enough buying power to profitably make any more trades. When you have a very small trading account or are going through a challenging losing period, another strategy is to focus exclusively on picking only the best stocks to trade. This is called "cherry picking."

For example, let's say there are five criteria that you normally use to pick the stocks you trade. When you cherry pick, you would trade only those stocks that meet all of the criteria. If you don't find stocks that meet all the criteria, you might sit on the sidelines for a while or decide to trade only the one or two that come the closest to meeting all the criteria. When we are cherry picking, we typically only trade the two or three best-looking stocks we can find.

To use this strategy, you must not execute every trade that looks good to you. You will need to study all of the technical data and select only those trades that have the best potential for a profit. This takes a little more studying and discipline, but it may well be worth your effort in the long run. Whether you are beginning with a small trading account or are stuck in a losing trading period, the cherry-picking strategy can help you make the most profitable use of your capital. If you force yourself to trade only the most potentially profitable trades, you can increase your percentage of profit and decrease the amount of your losses.

Learn the individual styles of the stocks you trade.

When we first began trading, we assumed that every stock traded in basically the same manner. It took a long time and a lot of money before we realized that every stock has a different trading style. Learning the particular style, or trading pattern, of a stock helps you understand and anticipate its short-term price movements, based on how it typically is traded by the market makers or specialists.

There are several things to look for and study with stocks you trade:

▸ The typical spread (difference between the bid and ask prices).
▸ The average trading range (range between the intra-day low and high prices).
▸ The types of pullbacks and bounces the stock typically has.

The typical spread

The spread is simply the price difference between the best bid price and the best ask or offer price. For example, if the best bid price of a stock is 50 3/8 and the best offer price is 50 5/8, then the stock would be trading with a 1/4-point spread.

If you learn to identify the typical spread that a stock trades with, you will begin to know whether the stock is acting normally or whether there is price manipulation. It also allows you to gauge buying or selling interest. For example, if the stock normally trades with a 1/8-point spread on a typical day, then you know something is odd with the stock if it starts trading with a 3/8-point spread. It means either there are fewer sellers—keeping the ask price up—or there are fewer buyers—keeping the bid price down. These can be clues to the possible direction the stock will take in the short term. On the other hand, if the stock is trading the whole day with its typical 1/8-point spread, then we are more inclined to believe it will trade as it normally does.

The average trading range

The average trading range could be described as the average range between the intra-day low price and the intra-day high price. For example, if a stock's intra-day low price is $78 and its intra-day high price is $83, then it would have a 5-point trading range for that particular day. The actual price that the stock closes at is not really relevant. The range is simply the difference between the low and the high of the day.

It is important to learn the average trading ranges of the stocks you trade because it enables you to notice changes in implied volatility. If the intra-day range of a stock seems to be increasing, then the stock is becoming more volatile. If it is decreasing, then the stock is becoming less volatile. These changes will play an important role in ultimately deciding your ideal entry and exit points. For us, the more volatile the stock, the better a trading stock it is.

The easiest way to determine average-trading ranges is to look at what is called a candlestick chart. There are many sites on the Internet that allow you to see candlestick charts of stocks, but one of our favorites is *www.bigcharts.com*. If you go to this site, you can view candlestick charts of any stock. There are also many great books on candlestick charting, which you can study for more in-depth analysis techniques.

Typical pullbacks and rallies

Perhaps one of the most important factors to study is how a stock typically reacts to sell-offs (also known as pullbacks) and rallies. No two stocks will ever react the same way. Some stocks will pull back by an average of 1/4 point, while others will pull back several points during the course of the day. Likewise, some stocks will only run 1/2 point before leveling off, while others will run several points.

Unfortunately, there is no easy way to determine the way individual stocks react to selling and buying other than to watch them trade throughout the day, if possible, or to consult intra-day charts at the end of the day. It is very hard to describe in words the different ways stocks react to rallies and sell-offs, and it is something that can only be assessed through studying each stock you trade.

The trend is your friend.

Before entering any trade, the first thing we do is identify the current short-term trend of the overall market. Although there are several types of market indexes, the Dow Jones Industrial Average is perhaps the most commonly followed. If you were planning on trading NASDAQ stocks, of course, you would track the NASDAQ Composite Index. The whole idea of following these indexes is to identify which way the market has been going for the past several weeks. There are three basic types of trends that the market will always be in: uptrend, downtrend, and sideways (also known as flat).

Uptrending market

An uptrending market is one that has been steadily growing during the last few days or weeks. This does not mean it has had no down days, it merely means that as a general trend, the stocks have been climbing. One key to identifying an uptrend in the market is to look at the Dow for higher highs and higher lows. This means that when the market runs up, each high it makes should generally be higher than the previous high it set. Likewise, each low the market makes when it pulls back should be higher than its previous low. If these things occur, it is safe to say that the market is uptrending.

If the market is uptrending you should, in general, try to be long in the stocks that have the most relative strength. If you are shorting stocks in an uptrending market, you need to make sure you use tight stop losses to protect your profits and take profits more quickly than if you were going long. In addition, you need to make sure the stocks you are shorting are weak relative to the market. As a rule, you should you are shorting are weak relative to the market. As a rule, you should never try to short strong stocks in an uptrend. Also, make sure that the stocks you are shorting are in weak sectors.

Downtrending market

A downtrending market is one that has steadily been declining during the last several days or weeks. This does not mean that there will be no up days. It merely means that the markets will be steadily going lower as a general trend. One key to identifying a downtrend in the market is to look at the Dow for lower highs and lower lows. This means that as the market is going down, each bounce to the upside should generally be a lower bounce than the previous one. Likewise, each low the market makes when it pulls back should be lower than the previous low. If these things occur, it is safe to say that the market is downtrending.

If the market is downtrending, you should try to short the stocks that have the most relative weakness. By going with the overall trend of the market, you will reduce your risk and maximize your profits. However, if you decide to go long on stocks in a downtrending market, you need to make sure you use tight stop losses and take profits more quickly than if you were going short. This will reduce your risk of trading against the trend.

Sideways market

A sideways market is also known as a flat market or a market that is stuck in a trading range. This means that the market is failing to make new highs and failing to set lower lows. In other words, the market is going back down when it hits previous resistance points, and bouncing back up when it hits the support levels. An example of this can be seen by looking at a chart for the Dow from May through September of 1999.

In a sideways market, the best way to trade is to hedge yourself by having some stocks that you are long and other stocks that you are short. That way, no matter which way the market decides to move, you are reducing your risk. Go long on the stocks with the most relative strength and go short on stocks that have the most relative weakness. In addition, it is important to make sure you take your profits quickly and not be greedy, as you may be in a trending market. A flat market may break out to the upside or downside at any time and you never know which way it will go. Protect your profits!

It is important to know what trend the market is in because you are less likely to have large losses and more likely to have larger gains. While it is possible to make money by fighting the trend, there is more money to be made and less risk to be had by going with the overall market trend.

Remember that you will also make more money by trading in both up *and* down markets by going both long *and* short, depending on the trend. So, don't stop trading when the market is in a downtrend. Instead, go short. Then, when the market is going up, go long. By doing so, you can make money both ways.

For us and many other traders, one of the toughest rules to follow is to go with the general trend of the market. There have been many situations where we entered a trade that we initially thought was a good one based on relative strength and volume, but then quickly decided we had made a bad move. How could this happen? After all, we did all the right things and we followed all the rules that we set for the trades we entered. So what went wrong? We tried to fight the overall trend of the market.

Is it possible to make money by trading stocks that are going against the trend? Sure! After all, the whole concept of trading by relative strength is that you are trading stocks that show strength relative to the market. However, the risk level does greatly increase by trading against the market. If you are long in a stock that is holding steady as the market is dropping, that is a good thing, but it may eventually drop or it may just sit flat. If you are short the market as the market is dropping, however, you are more likely to make money.

Look for trend reversals on daily charts and trade them.

As we discussed above, a stock will always fall into one of three types of trends. It will either be in an uptrend, a downtrend, or in a flat trading range. Knowing how to identify these trends is a crucial element of trading based on trends. Obviously, no stock will ever go in a totally straight line up or a straight line down. There will always be dips or pullbacks and spikes or rallies, regardless of what type of trend the stock is in. This is easily identifiable by looking at the daily chart of any particular stock. In other words, you can generally determine the current trend for a particular stock by studying the daily charts for that stock.

For example, if you look at chart 1 on page 87, you will see a stock that is in an uptrend. Note the higher highs and higher lows. Notice the straight lines we were able to draw that illustrate the uptrend. Another trait you will frequently see in an uptrending stock is an increase in the average daily volume. Looking at the volume bars on the bottom of the chart, notice how the volume of the stock increases each time the price of the stock gets higher. That is an indication that the stock is gaining more and more interest as time goes by.

If you look at chart 2 on page 88, you will see a stock that is in a downtrend. Note the lower highs and lower lows. Even though the stock has had some rallies that caused the price to rise, the high price of the rally was not able to go higher than the previous high. Likewise, the stock is setting a lower price each time it sells off. You will also notice that the volume of the stock is increasing as the price drops. (The straight lines illustrate the downtrend.)

Looking at chart 3 on page 89, you will see a stock that is stuck in a trading range, also known as being sideways. A trading range means that the stock is not trending higher, nor is it trending lower. It is just staying flat. Unlike the higher highs, higher lows, lower highs, and lower lows that we discussed earlier, a flat stock stays stuck between its current high prices *and* its low prices. When the stock rallies, the price goes to the previous high price, but then pulls

Chart 1: Uptrend

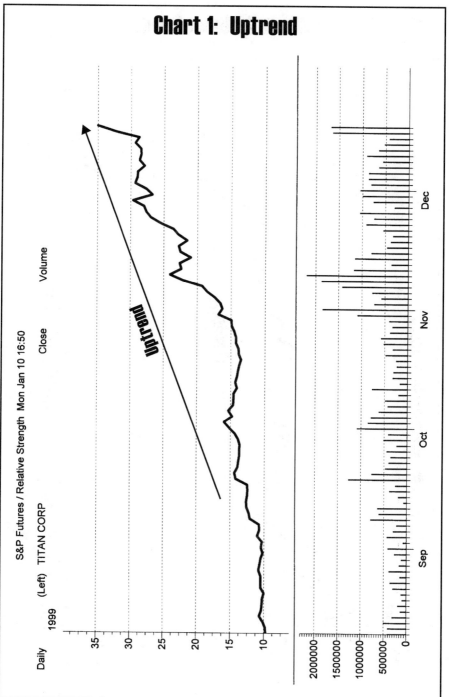

S&P Futures / Relative Strength Mon Jan 10 16:50

(Left) TITAN CORP   Close   Volume

Daily   1999

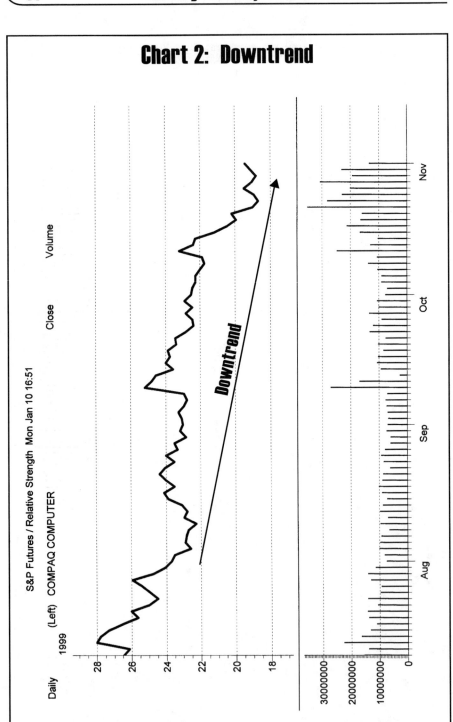

Chart 2: Downtrend

Chart 3: Trading range (sideways trend)

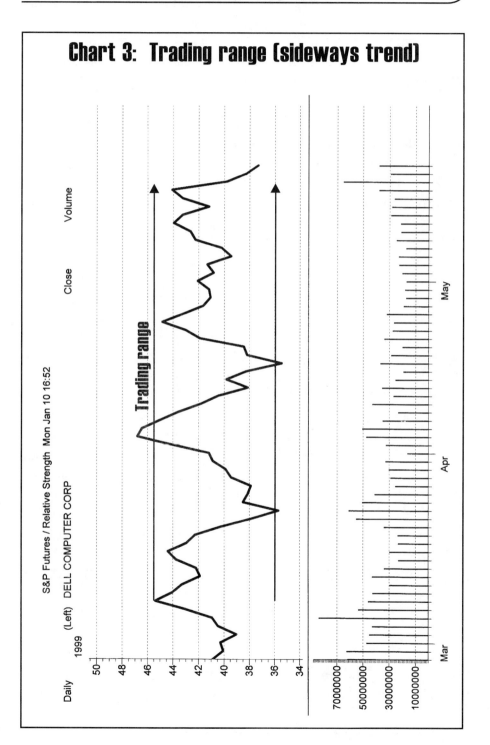

back down again once it reaches that price. When it sells off, it drops to the previous low price, but then bounces off of the low and goes back up to the previous high price.

If you are able to identify the trends of stocks based upon the above information, then it makes sense that it should be relatively simple to also identify trend reversals in stocks. The easiest way to identify changes in trends is to look for a reversing pattern of either higher highs and lows or lower highs and lows.

For example, if the stock was in an uptrend, it was setting higher highs and higher lows. But if the stock rallies and fails to reach the previous high that it set with its last rally, and then drops down below the previous low, it is a possible indication that the stock's trend could be reversing. Note that the operative word is possible. But before assuming that an uptrending stock has reversed direction, we always wait for confirmation. We wait for the next rally to see if the high price reaches the previous high, or if it again sets a lower high. If the stock sets a lower high for the second time in a row, then it is rather safe to assume that the stock has at least temporarily reversed direction.

Likewise, if a stock in a downtrend suddenly sets a price that is higher than its previous high, and then the new low price also becomes higher than the previous low, it is a possible indication that the trend has reversed. Again, we recommend waiting for confirmation of the trend reversal by waiting for the next rally and seeing if a higher price is again set.

As you may have guessed, there is a lot of money to be made by trading stocks in easily identifiable trend reversals. If you are able to quickly identify a trend reversal, you can either buy or sell short the stock before the majority of investors realize that it has changed direction. This will yield you higher profits and less risk. This is why we want you to know how to discern the various patterns you will see.

The basic concept is to buy stocks that are in uptrends and to sell short stocks that are in downtrends. In fact, the "trend is your friend" is a common saying among traders. Your stock, however, doesn't need to be in an uptrend to trade it. You can always make just as much money in a down market or downtrend as you can in an uptrend.

It is also possible to make money by trading stocks that are in trading ranges if you buy near the bottoms and sell short at the tops. However, the risk is greater in trading flat stocks because the stock could easily break out of its trading range and leave you with a significant and rapid loss if you are not totally cognizant of your stop losses. Therefore, at least for novice traders, we recommend that you stick to trading stocks that are in either an uptrend or a downtrend.

One other important thing to realize is that the trend of a stock is based on history. This means that there is never a guarantee that the stock will continue its trend in the future. As all disclaimers say, past performance is no guarantee of future results. Although this is true, remember that we are merely trying to put proven statistical market averages in our favor. Therefore, although we can never be assured that the near term trend of a stock will continue in the future, we at least want to put the odds in our favor. Always remember, though, that if the unexpected happens, it is crucial to use your stop losses.

Trade stocks with relative strength.

We believe there are several elements that go into deciding which stocks to trade, but a divergent stock pattern is one of the most important things to look for. A divergent stock pattern is simply an indicator of a stock's strength in relation to the major market indices it is a part of, typically the Dow, the NASDAQ, or the S&P 500. For this reason, we like to say that the extent of a divergent stock pattern indicates a stock's "relative strength" to the market. Relative strength is important because trading stocks that are showing relative strength reduces your risk while allowing you to maximize your gains. Following are several examples of divergent stock patterns.

The chart on page 93 shows the movement of both the Dow and International Paper (IP) for the period of October 8 to 14, 1999.

Notice that the Dow had a downward trend for this particular time period. On October 8, the Dow was at approximately 10,650, but it closed at approximately 10,280 on October 14. Therefore, the Dow Jones Average lost approximately 3.5 percent of its value for the period.

Now, take a look at International Paper's trend for the same time period. On October 8, IP was just over 47 1/2 per share, but it closed over $50 per share on October 14. International Paper gained approximately 5.5 percent in value for the period.

As the Dow Jones Average was going down, IP was going up. Because IP was moving steadily up as the market was going down, it is correct to say that IP had *relative strength* for this particular time period. If a stock has relative strength to the market, then that is a stock you want to consider buying. The first indication of the precise time to buy a particular stock is when you first notice the divergent pattern on the stock's chart.

By buying a stock that is showing relative strength, your risk for loss is greatly reduced because even if the entire stock market drops significantly, your stock will drop at a proportion that is much less. This is due to the relative strength that the stock is showing.

On the other hand, if the stock market has a strong rally, International Paper will go up at a higher proportion than the overall market because of its relative strength. If the stock is already strong to begin with, it will only get stronger as money is pouring into the market. But the nice part is, that even if the market doesn't rally, your risk for loss has been minimized. The whole concept is to minimize your risks while allowing the opportunity for maximum gains.

Chart five on page 94 shows the movement of both the NASDAQ Composite Average and Broadcom for the period of October 4 to 11, 1999.

Notice that the NASDAQ had an upward trend for this particular period of time. On October 4, the NASDAQ was approximately 2,797

Chart 4: Relative Strength

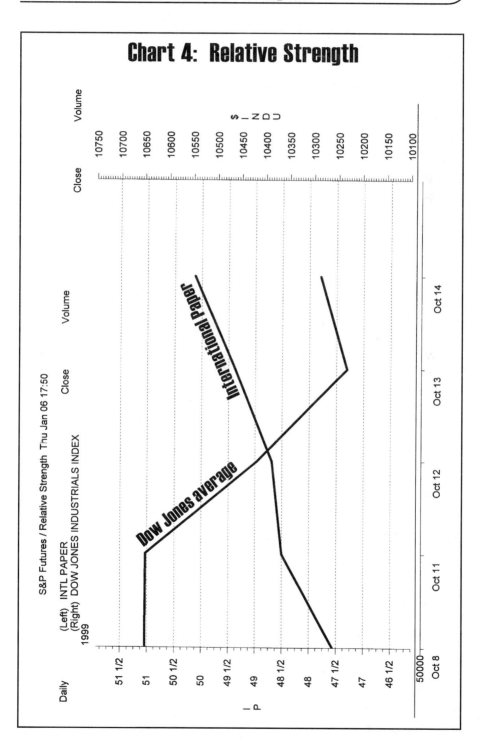

Chart 5: No relative strength

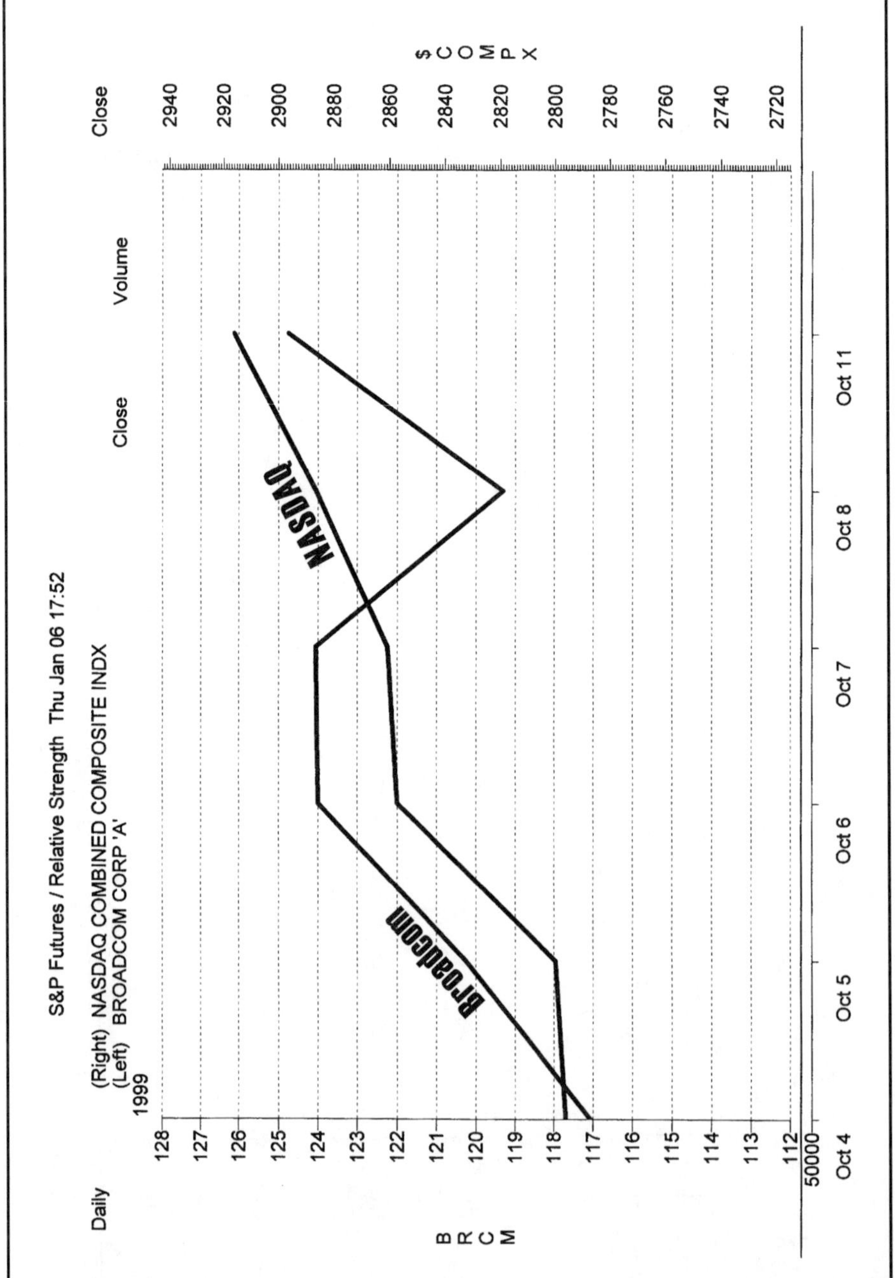

and it closed around 2,917 on October 11. Therefore, the NASDAQ Composite gained about 4.2 percent in value for this period.

Now, take a look at Broadcom's trend for the same time period. On October 4, Broadcom was at just under $117 per share. It closed at $125 per share on October 11. Therefore, Broadcom gained about 6 percent in value for the period.

The NASDAQ Composite went up about 4.2 percent for the week and Broadcom went up by approximately the same percentage (6 percent). In this example, it is correct to say that Broadcom had *no relative strength* for the period because Broadcom was basically moving with the market. When the market was up, Broadcom was up; when the market was down, so was Broadcom. There was no divergence.

If a stock is trading with the market, it is best not to trade the stock at all because the stock will go wherever the market goes, and we never know for certain which way the market is going to go. Although the market was up in this example, if it did decide to go down, the stock would most likely also go down. There is more risk by trading stocks that are trending with the market, that is, with no relative strength, due to the uncertainty of the future market direction as a whole. In this example, Broadcom is not a stock you would want to trade at this particular time.

The chart on page 96 shows the movement of both the Dow Jones Industrial Average and Coca-Cola Corporation for the period from September 23 to October 5, 1999.

Notice that the Dow had a modest uptrend for this particular period. On September 23, the Dow was about 10,320; it closed around 10,400 on October 5. Therefore, the Dow Jones Average gained about 1 percent in value for the time period.

Coca-Cola, however, did not fare as well. On September 23, Coke was around $51 per share, but it closed near $48 on October 5. Therefore, Coke actually lost about 6 percent of its value for the period. Although the Dow went up by about 1 percent, Coke actually lost 6

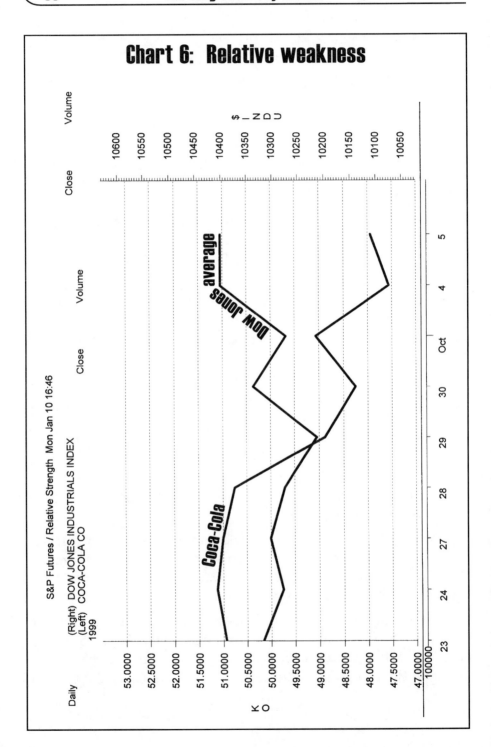

Chart 6: Relative weakness

percent of its value during the same period of time. There was a divergent stock pattern to the downside for Coca-Cola. Therefore, it is correct to say that Coke had *relative weakness* for this particular period. When a stock is exhibiting relative weakness, such as Coke in this example, the best thing to do is to short the stock. Remember that we want to make money with the market going both ways.

You can see that Coke was very weak because it was steadily going down even as the market was rallying. If the market suddenly changed direction and started dropping, Coke would probably quickly drop proportionately more than the market because it was a weak stock to begin with. A weak market would only cause it to drop more. This is a good example of a stock that you may have wanted to short for this time period. The first indication to short the stock would be the divergent pattern of the stock as the market was rallying.

Trade stocks that have broken support or resistance levels.

One of the most challenging concepts of day trading is knowing exactly when to enter into a position or buy a stock based on technical indicators. If you read a book devoted to the technical analysis of stocks, you will find all kinds of interesting terms and concepts that are very complex and even hard to pronounce, such as MACD, stochastics, or Fibonacci lines. Obviously, there is a place for all of these indicators—otherwise they would not exist—however, we are here to tell you that you really do not need them in order to profit as a short-term trader. Our personal trading results have proven that time and again. There are, of course, several technical indicators that are crucial to understand. The good news is that they are relatively easy to identify and comprehend.

Support Levels

A support level is the price at which the stock finds buying interest that ends up preventing the stock from going below the previous low price that the stock set. Typically, a support level tends to be the price that a stock will bounce off of, based on past results. People will often buy a stock at a support level because they think they are getting the best possible price. Essentially, investors and traders feel they have the best chance for a large return and the lowest risk by buying stocks that are at or near their previous support levels. Also, support levels tend to exist because people that are short the stock also tend to cover around support levels. This causes a wave of buying in the stock, which makes the price rise. Let's look at Johnson & Johnson's activity for a six-month period in 1999, as an example (page 99).

In this chart, you will see that each time the price of the stock dropped to about $90 or $91, it failed to go any lower and quickly bounced to a higher price. Therefore, you would say that there is support at $90 or $91.

Resistance Levels

The opposite of support levels are resistance levels. A resistance level is the price at which a stock tends to weaken and pull back to a price lower than the previous high. A resistance level tends to be the price at which a stock is unable to break higher. This occurs in large part because of a large number of sellers who tend to show up at resistance points. These sellers fit into two categories.

In the first category are people who are selling short when the stock reaches a resistance level because they are betting on the fact that the stock will drop back down again. In the second category of sellers are those people who previously bought the stock at a high price, then had a loss when the stock sold off, and now are anxious to just get out of the stock at a break-even price. Therefore, they end up selling when the stock reaches its former high price, which forms technical resistance.

If you look again at Johnson & Johnson's chart, you will notice that the stock also tends to drop to a lower price each time it goes to the high of about $105-106. Therefore, the resistance level for this same stock is around $105 or $106. Not only is this chart a good example of support and resistance levels, but is also a good example of a stock that is in a sideways trend, or stuck in a trading range.

Chart 7: Support and resistance levels

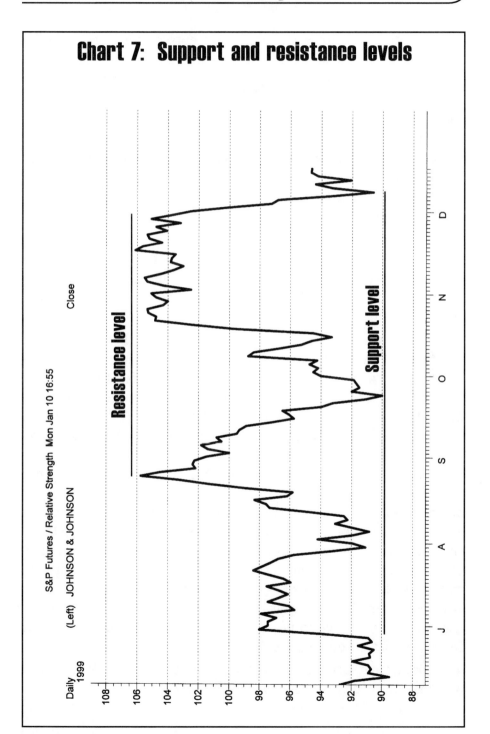

S&P Futures / Relative Strength Mon Jan 10 16:55

(Left) JOHNSON & JOHNSON   Close

Daily
1999

Now that you understand the concepts of support and resistance levels, what exactly do you do with this information? Essentially, the key here is to trade what are called the "breakouts."

A breakout occurs when a stock that had previously been encountering either resistance or support suddenly breaks through the resistance or support that it was previously encountering. If a stock breaks through a resistance point, then it is a breakout to the upside. If the stock breaks below a support point, then it is a breakout to the downside, also known as a breakdown. Remember: Money can be made either way, up or down.

One of our favorite methods of making several points of profit is to buy stocks that have broken out. This method of trading is highly profitable because it often works statistically and it has minimal risk if you use stop losses. Take a look at chart 8 on page 101, which is a chart for Prodigy Communications Corporation (PRGY).

You will notice that before October 29, 1999, there was a lot of resistance at the price of around $22. The stock tried to break above that price several times, but each time it was met with sellers and consequently dropped down below that price. But notice what happened to the stock as the volume started to increase. On October 29, Prodigy traded past $22, and quickly went up to $25. The increasing volume was a sign that the stock was likely to break through the resistance level of $22. As soon as it safely passed the resistance point of $22, we bought the stock at a price of 22 1/4. Why did we do this? Because we knew that if the stock traded above its resistance point on high volume, most of the sellers would be gone, and the shorts that were left would be forced to cover, driving the price even higher. By the end of the day on October 29, Prodigy had traded up to a high price of over $25. Were we surprised? Not at all. When we entered the trade at 22 1/4, we were 90 percent confident that we would be able to make at least a several-point profit on it. Indeed, it turned out to be quite a profitable trade for us.

For another example of buying breakouts, take a look at chart 9 on page 103, which is a chart for Coca-Cola (KO).

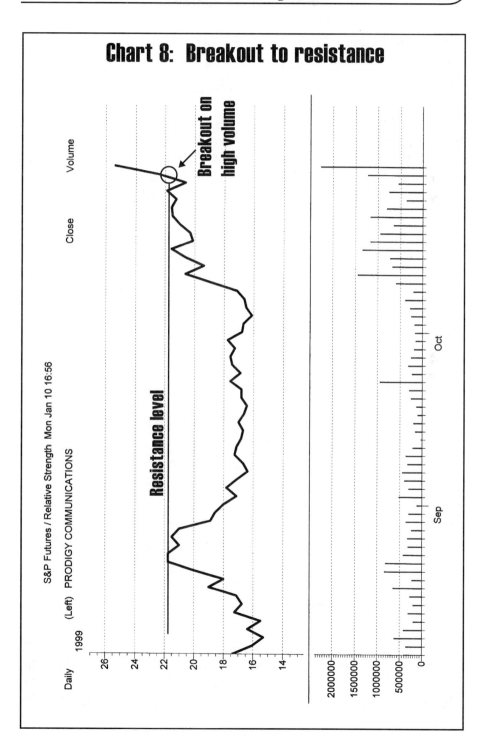

Chart 8: Breakout to resistance

S&P Futures / Relative Strength Mon Jan 10 16:56

Daily (Left) PRODIGY COMMUNICATIONS

1999   Close   Volume

Resistance level

Breakout on high volume

Before October 21, 1999, there was a lot of resistance at the price of $53 to $54. Notice how the stock was in a downtrend prior to that date, which caused a lot of selling and heavy resistance every time the stock started to rally. On several occasions prior to October 21, Coke tried to go higher than the $54 price, but was met with resistance and dropped back down. However, notice that the low price it dropped to after the first run to the resistance level of $53 to $54 was actually higher than the previous low price. In other words, the first low price was around $48, but after trading up to $54, the new low only went down to about $51 (around October 13). This was our first clue of a possible trend reversal—a higher low. So when it came back up to test the resistance level of $54 again, we were confident that the stock would break through that resistance point and go higher. That is exactly what happened. We bought KO at 54 3/ 8, and it proceeded to run up to $59 over the course of the next three days because it broke through the resistance. You would have made an easy 4 points if you had bought the breakout at $54. But remember to always wait for the breakout to actually happen before buying the stock. If we had bought at $53 instead of $54, the stock could just as easily have gone right back down to the $51 range, which would have caused us to get "stopped out." Once again, it turned out to be quite a profitable trade for us, with minimal risk. Starting to get the idea of how buying the breakouts works?

The opposite concept applies with stocks that break below their support levels. If a stock you are following suddenly fails to bounce off of its previous support level and falls below that price, then that stock becomes a candidate for possibly shorting. But, again, wait until the next rally to see if the stock also sets a lower high. Then short into that rally to get the best price.

One very important point, however, is that you should not buy the stock until it actually trades above its resistance point. If you buy the stock before it breaks through its resistance point, you are taking a big risk that it will simply trade up to its resistance point and come back down to a lower price, thereby forcing you to use your stop loss. Although you will end up paying a higher price if you wait for the

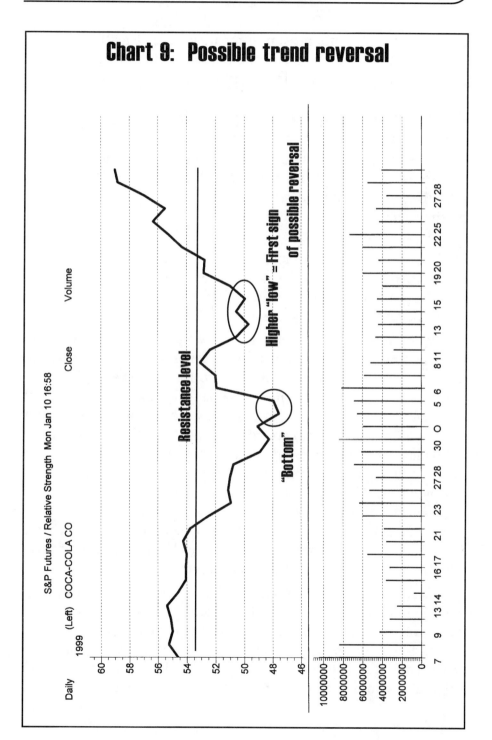

Chart 9: Possible trend reversal

stock to break past its resistance point, it doesn't matter. You will end up making more money in the long term due to the decreased risk. Always wait for the stock to break out—don't gamble!

Understand and use the risk/reward ratio.

Do you want a really easy way to minimize your risk when trading stocks? Then you definitely need to learn about the risk/reward ratio. Understanding this basic concept will minimize your risks and maximize your profits.

Considering the risk/reward ratio of a trade means being aware of the risk of the trade compared to the possible reward. In other words, what is the downside risk compared to the upside potential? If there appears to be more downside risk than profit potential, don't make the trade. If the opposite is true, then proceed.

When we day trade, this is a factor we are constantly weighing. One good example for a short-term trader is with a stock that has already run up many points for the day. Let's say the stock has already risen from $40 per share to $47 per share during the course of one trading day. If we decide to buy this stock at a price of $47, what would you say is our risk/reward? We would say that the downside risk is much greater than the upside potential, because the stock is more likely to go down several dollars than go up. We are risking more money on the downside in an attempt to gain a mere dollar or so of profit on the upside. However, if we had entered this stock at a price of around $42, the risk/reward ratio would have been much more favorable because the stock would only have been up $2 at that time; it would have had much more upside potential.

Let's look at another example of risk/reward. Suppose you are considering buying two stocks. One broke its 52-week high a week ago and has had five consecutive days of gains since then. Therefore, it is sitting at its new 52-week high again. The other is nearing its 52-week high level, with increasing volume to the upside, but has not yet traded above that number. In the short term, all other factors being equal, which one of these two trades do you feel would have the better risk/reward ratio? If you chose the second example, you are correct.

In the first example, it is extremely likely that the stock will be due for some profit-taking and will quickly turn around in the other direction. If you bought that stock, you could potentially lose a significant amount of money, due to the strong runup that the stock just had. The upside profit potential is also more limited because the stock has already run a lot.

In the second example, we would say the risk/reward ratio is much better because your downside is not as great in the first example. But, more importantly, your upside profit potential is much greater. Remember that once this stock breaks its former 52-week high, it is likely to keep going several points higher before turning back around. Therefore, in this example, although there is still downside risk, the upside potential is much greater.

Understanding the risk/reward ratio concept is crucial because it enables you to decide which trades have the least risk and the most profit potential. This especially comes in handy if you find several stocks that all appear to be fundamentally good stocks to enter, but you can only afford to buy one of them. The deciding factor can be based upon the risk/reward ratio of each stock. A stock that you feel has upside potential of $5 per share and that appears to have a minimal downside risk of $1 or so—based on the fact that it is trading near a technical support level—would probably be a good trade to enter. One in which you are risking $7 to $10 on the downside in an attempt to gain $2 per share on the upside would probably not.

Unfortunately, there is no concrete or objective way to determine risk/reward for each trade. It is more a matter of using common sense and basic technical analysis. Remember to always look at technical support and resistance levels to help you determine your risk/reward for entering any position.

Do not select a stock based on price alone.

When we first began our trading careers, we were working with very limited capital, and were concerned that we would not have enough to profitably day trade stocks. As a result, we looked for very inexpensive stocks to trade. The stocks we traded were typically priced anywhere from $3 to $20 per share. Our rationale for selecting these low-priced stocks was that we would be able to afford to buy more shares and, therefore, make more profit. At the time, that reasoning sounded quite logical, and we even made some profit by trading those low-priced issues. But we failed to realize one crucial point. There was just as much profit to be made by trading higher priced stocks, because the higher priced stocks move proportionately more on a point basis. Therefore, we could make as much profit buying fewer shares of an expensive stock as we could buying more shares of a less expensive stock. Let's look at some examples to illustrate our point.

Example 1: Let's say you decide to buy 500 shares of a stock that is priced at $10 per share. Excluding commission, it would cost you $5,000. If that stock moves up 5 percent in value, you are looking at a gain of 50 cents per share, which would now price the stock at $10.50 per share, giving you a value of $5,250. Therefore, the net result is a gain of $250 on capital of $5,000.

Example 2: You decide to buy an expensive stock with your $5,000. It costs $125 per share, so you only buy 40 shares. The stock then increases 5 percent in value, as in the previous example. A 5 percent gain gives you a gain of $6.25 per share, which now prices the stock at $131.25 per share. Your investment now totals $5,250, or $131.25 per share times 40 shares. Therefore, your net profit is $250 on capital of $5,000.

As you can see from these examples, when a stock moves a given percentage up or down, your profit potential is not affected in any way by the number of shares you bought. A 5 percent gain is the same profit whether the stock is cheap or expensive. The point here is not to get fooled into thinking that you can't make as much money by buying fewer expensive stocks because it really makes no difference. Expensive stocks will proportionately move more points than small stocks, but when you look at the gains in terms of percentages, the end results will always be the same.

Although there is nothing wrong with buying stocks that are inexpensive and meet all the other criteria, make sure you don't limit yourself to buying only inexpensive stocks. If your capital is limited, you may indeed feel kind of silly buying only 25 shares of a stock. We sure did. But if that $200 stock moves 10 points, you just made $250 profit. Don't be deceived into thinking you need to buy lots of shares to make money. Obviously, this is ideal, but you can also make money with fewer shares of more expensive stocks.

Avoid stocks that are about to announce earnings.

In early 1998, we decided to take a chance on buying some shares of Yahoo! (YHOO) right before earnings for the stock were about to be released. So, a day before the earnings announcement, we bought our position and then anxiously waited for the earnings release. The next day's earnings results were fabulous. Yahoo! not only met its estimates, it beat them by nearly 20 percent. The company had nothing but huge revenue and growth increases to report. Our heads filled with thoughts of dollar signs. We thought we were so smart to know Yahoo! was going to have excellent earnings. We slept very well that night, satisfied that we would wake up to a nice profit. Unfortunately, that wasn't what happened the next morning.

Within 15 minutes of the market's opening, Yahoo! was already trading down a whopping 9 points from the previous day's close. Our hearts sank. Five days later, Yahoo! was down approximately 30 points! Our stop loss kicked in, and we took a major hit. We could have held onto it and it would have eventually come back, but remember, we need to play by the rules so that we can stay in the game until the next day.

So what happened? Obviously, the pros on Wall Street must have felt that the current valuation of the stock had already factored in superb earnings, and they therefore sold off the stock, despite the good news. Likewise, there are just as many times when a stock will run sky high on a less-than-stellar earnings report.

The moral of the story? Avoid being in stocks that are about to announce earnings because it is impossible to determine which direction the stock will go after earnings are released. Ask any experienced trader and we are sure he or she will tell you many similar stories. Trading stocks that are about to announce earnings is the same as gambling. If you want to gamble, go to Las Vegas. The goal we are trying to accomplish is to teach you how to maximize your profit while minimizing your risk. Trading stocks that are about to announce earnings is certainly not the way to do that.

Trade stocks in the strongest or weakest sectors.

One method of trading often overlooked by novice traders is called sector trading. This means that you do not trade individual stocks at random, but rather you trade stocks within the strongest market sectors if you are going long, and the weakest sectors if you are going short. One phenomenon we have noticed during our years of trading is that money is constantly being shifted from sector to sector, regardless of current market conditions. We have noticed that on any given day or week, there will always be one or two very strong sectors. Sometimes it is the oil sector, sometimes it is the tech sector, and sometimes it is the pharmaceutical sector. We believe this is a result of the constant shifting of large amounts of money by mutual fund managers into various sectors. This is also why sectors that have the most relative strength or weakness will also tend to be the sectors that are showing higher-than-average volume. Remember that we are looking for sectors that are showing not only strength or weakness, but, more importantly, higher-than-average volume. High volume indicates true buying or selling interest in a particular sector.

One benefit to sector trading is that your overall risk in the market seems to be lower than if you were just trading stocks at random in various sectors. By being in the sectors that are the strongest, you are basically going with the trend, and not fighting it. Whenever you go with the trend, you are always more likely to make money because you are doing what the big money is doing.

Another benefit to sector trading is that your average gains will tend to be larger because you have momentum on your side. If you are able to identify sectors that are strong before everyone else identifies them, your gains will be considerably higher because of the follow-through momentum that typically occurs in strong sectors. We have found that buying or selling momentum in a sector will usually last for about three days. If you are able to identify these shifts in momentum in the beginning, you will be able to make more gains.

Earlier in the book, we talked about trading individual stocks that are showing the most strength relative to the overall markets. Although you can trade virtually any stock that is showing relative strength, the odds of a profitable trade are more in your favor if you stick to trading stocks that are in individual sectors with the most relative strength and higher-than-average volume. If the sector is showing relative strength or weakness, but not higher-than-average volume, the sector may not truly be as strong or as weak as you think. Volume tells the true picture of a sector's strength or weakness.

The easiest way to identify sectors with relative strength or weakness is to consult a chart that will allow you to see an overlay of any sector compared to the Dow, NASDAQ, or S&P 500. Our favorite place to do this is at *www.marketwatch.com*. They have charting features that allow you to compare various sectors with the either the Dow, NASDAQ, or any other market index.

If we are going long, we look for sectors that are in an uptrend at a pace that is better than the Dow Jones average. There are several key factors to look for in order to identify this. We will walk you through the various factors that we look for when comparing sectors.

First, we will typically look at a line chart that has a period of 90 days displayed. Although you can easily use a one-year chart, we have found that a 90-day chart gives a more accurate picture of what has actually transpired during the most recent time period. Remember, we are trading stocks that we generally intend to only be in for several days to a week. Therefore, the long-term trend of a sector is not nearly as important as the short-term trend. Remember that we are not investing.

Second, we look at the relative strength of the sectors. When doing so, we will look at pullbacks in the market. How did the sector react whenever the market sold off? Typically, the sector will do one of three things when the market sells off:

1. The sector will sell off at a pace corresponding to the overall market.
2. The sector will not sell off much, but will also not rally at all. In other words, the sector will stay flat.
3. The sector will actually rise in price as the market is selling off.

Out of the three options above, which one do you think presents the best opportunity for going long in a sector? If you guessed the third option, you are correct. Number three would be the sector with the most relative strength because as the market was selling off, the sector was actually rallying. Therefore, when the market stops selling off and starts to rally again, guess what that sector is going to do now? It will explode to the upside. Why? Because if it had enough buyers interested even as the market was selling off, imagine how many more buyers will show up once the market starts to rally. So, based on relative strength alone, the best sector to go long in is the sector that shows the most upward strength whenever the market pulls back. Remember also that volume is a key element to consider. Make sure that the stock has increasing average daily volume as it is rallying.

If you are going short on a sector, you would look for the opposite traits. In order to go short, you want the market to be in a general downtrend. Then, whenever the market bounces, you look to see how the sectors react to the rallies in the market. If you are going short, you obviously want to short the sectors that are showing the most negative relative "relative weakness." When the market bounces, which sectors do not bounce, and even continue down, even though the market is going up? Those are the best sectors to go short with. The most ideal time to go short in these sectors is when the market bounces—this insures that you will get the best price for your short.

Trade a basket of stocks within each sector you are trading.

In our opinion, one of the most profitable and least risky trading techniques is to trade a "basket" of stocks within each sector that you have chosen to trade. This means that instead of trading just one stock within a sector that you have identified to be strong, you trade at least two or three stocks within that sector. Just as professional money managers and mutual fund managers recommend diversifying your stocks, the same concept is applied here within each sector. There are two main benefits to trading a basket of stocks: more profit and lower risk. You will consistently achieve a higher percentage of profit and lower your risk by trading a basket of stocks within a sector. Let's look at a few examples of why this is so.

Suppose you have identified that the airline sector is weak because it is showing a lot of downward momentum and negative relative strength. So, you decide to go short on American Airlines (AMR). Now, if you only have this one short position, you are basically at the mercy of this stock's performance. If it drops, you make a profit when you cover. If it stays flat, you break even. If it runs up, you cut your loss and lose money. But, either way, your fate is determined solely by the performance of this one stock.

Let's look at a different approach to the above scenario. You still want to go short in the airline sector, but this time you decide to go short on a basket of stocks within the sector. You sell short American Airlines (AMR), Delta (DAL), and Continental (CAL). There are a couple of possible outcomes to doing this. Let's suppose that DAL drops 1 point, CAL drops 2 points, and AMR drops 1 point. If that happens, you are pretty happy. You covered all three positions and you netted a 4-point profit.

Another scenario is that DAL drops 1 point, CAL drops 1 point, and AMR goes up 1 point, forcing you to cover and take a loss. If that happens, you are still looking at a 1-point profit, even though you lost money on AMR, since the loss on AMR is compensated for by the profit on CAL. So, those two stocks (AMR and CAL) give you a net result of being even. But you still made a 1-point gain on DAL. However, if you had been trading AMR, like in the first example, you would actually have had a 1-point loss.

The last scenario is that DAL stays flat, CAL drops 1 point, and AMR goes up 1 point, again causing a 1-point loss. If that happens, even though you took a 1-point loss on AMR, you are still basically even, minus commissions, because the profit you made on CAL makes up for the loss on AMR, and you broke even on DAL.

As you can see by the preceding examples, the profit potential is greater with trading a basket of stocks. Instead of making a profit on only one stock, you can end up making a profit on several stocks. A 1-point gain on one stock is obviously a profit of 1 point. However, that same 1-point gain on three different stocks now becomes a 3-point gain. Basically, you are able to triple your potential for profit, but still be looking for only a 1-point gain on each stock.

When deciding which stocks to trade within a sector, make sure you always select the leaders of each sector, not the laggards. The leaders of each sector will typically move more than the laggards each time the sector moves. It is important to understand that the leaders will typically have the highest average volume, be the most volatile, and move the most points each time the sector moves. Don't make the mistake of trading the laggards and thinking that because they haven't moved as much as the leaders, they are more likely to catch up to the leaders. What typically happens when you trade the laggards of each sector is that they will start out barely moving and will not pick up any momentum. They typically end up being the laggards at the end of a sector rally as well.

Leaders, on the other hand, typically start out moving nicely and pick up stronger and stronger momentum as the sector gains strength. Don't think that you are getting a better deal by buying the laggards because they are cheaper. Although the leaders of each sector cost more to buy, they will typically also yield the highest profit when you trade them. Always stick to trading the leaders of each sector.

The one common trait that we look for when trading sectors is higher-than-average volume. Again, you need to make sure that there is always higher-than-average volume present in each sector you are trading. This is true whether you are going long or selling short. Remember, the more volume in the group, the more confirmation that there is true relative strength or weakness. Don't underestimate the power of trading stocks that are showing higher-than-average volume.

Because it is unlikely that you would end up with a loss on each and every stock within your basket of stocks, your risk is minimized because the profitable trades will make up for any losing trades within your basket. Even if you are unable to make a profit with each and every stock in your basket, you can usually still end up with a profit because of the diversity.

Trade the largest and most volatile stocks within each sector.

Now that you understand the importance of sector trading and buying baskets of stocks, you may be wondering how to decide which individual stocks to trade within each sector. Ultimately, you will end up trading the stocks that have the most relative strength, along with stocks that have broken support and resistance levels, and stocks showing changes in trends. However, it is helpful to know where to start when deciding which stocks within a sector to trade.

Whenever we decide to trade a particular sector, we always trade the same stocks within that sector. The primary benefit of this, as we mentioned earlier in the book, is that you are able to learn the pattern and style of the specialist or market makers that trade each stock. Again, you will find that you get better at trading certain stocks simply through the experience of learning how that stock trades. But, how do you know which ones to trade on a regular basis?

The first thing that we look for within each sector are the stocks that tend to be the most volatile. As a short-term trader, know that volatility is your friend. It is obviously much more difficult to make money in a stock that only has an average intra-day trading range of 1 point, compared to a stock that has an average trading range of 2 to 3 points.

Within the computer-maker sector, Compaq (CPQ) is a good example of a stock that we do not trade. Typically it will only move about 1 point or less in either direction each day it trades, unless of course there is news affecting the stock that day. On the other hand, a stock like Gateway (GTW) is much easier to make a profit with because it typically will move at least 2 to 4 points in either direction during the course of one day. It is much easier to make a profit by trading a stock that will move 2 to 4 points than it is with a stock that moves only 1 point. The interesting thing is that typical investors, unlike short-term traders, do not like volatility because it makes them nervous when the value of their portfolio changes quickly. However, volatility is your best friend when you are short-term trading. That is why you need to trade the most volatile stocks within each sector.

One way to identify the volatility of a stock is to look at a table that lists the trading range of a stock for every day that it trades. If you go to the Yahoo! finance site (*www.yahoo.com*), you will be able to not only display charts of any stock, but you will also be able to display a table that lists data for each day that any stock has traded. You will find information such as the intra-day trading range (which is the key to seeing volatility), volume, opening price, and closing price for each day. You can even download the tables in spreadsheet format so that you can print them out and study them.

In addition to volatility, we also look for stocks that have the largest market capitalization and the largest floats, meaning the number of shares available to be traded. Stocks that have a large market cap and large floats are what we refer to as large stocks.

The primary benefit to trading large stocks is that they tend to move in a more logical and orderly fashion than their smaller counterparts. This is caused by several factors. First of all, large stocks tend to have more institutional and investor money that flows into and out of them, as opposed to Internet stocks, which are largely affected by day traders. When a stock has a lot of institutional and investor interest, it will typically move in a particular direction for a longer period of time than if a bunch of day traders suddenly decided to buy it for whatever reason. Therefore, you are less likely to have a technically good trade, such as buying a breakout, ruined by some inexperienced day traders who interrupt the orderly progression of the stock movement.

Although no stock could be said to truly move in a logical fashion, there is no doubt in our mind that stocks with large floats and large market caps move more as one would expect them to. If they start the day out strong, they will frequently remain that way throughout the remainder of the day. The same is true if they start out the day weak.

Another benefit of trading large stocks is that the spreads or the difference between the bid and the offer prices are typically much lower than those stocks that are less liquid. Instead of a 1/2-point spread, you are usually looking at a 1/8- or 1/4-point spread. This allows you to enter and exit the stocks at a better price and with less effort.

The last thing we look for are stocks that have an average daily volume of at least 500,000 to 1,000,000 shares traded. This is important because high average volume provides the crucial liquidity needed to absorb the big blocks that are commonly traded with individual stocks. For example, if you are long a stock that only trades an average of 100,000 shares a day, what do you think would happen if one block trade of 50,000 shares comes through on the sell side? Most likely, the stock would drop significantly due to the lack of liquidity. However, if you are long a stock that trades an average of 5 million shares a day, and a 50,000-share block sale comes through, the stock would probably hardly be affected, if at all. In fact, it may only cause the stock to drop by a 1/4-point or so, compared to a possible several-point drop on a less liquid issue. To put it simply, a large block could result in a big move (often in the wrong direction) for a stock that is not liquid enough. Volume is the key!

So when selecting stocks to trade within a particular sector, the three most important factors to look for are volatility, volume, and size. Also, of course, make sure there is relative strength. Relative strength is always the primary trait we look for. Although this may sound time consuming, you will quickly begin to learn which stocks are the best ones to trade if you pay attention to the major stocks in each sector. Once you identify these stocks, make a list of them so that you can trade those same stocks whenever you are trading that sector.

In case you are curious, here is a list of some of the major sectors and individual stocks within those sectors that we frequently trade, in no particular order. Note that the list is certainly not all-inclusive:

Oil:	XOM, BPA, CHV, TX
Pharmaceutical:	MRK, JNJ, AMGN, LLY, PFE
Banks:	CMB, AXP, C, BAC, FTU
Semiconductor:	TXN, MOT, INTC, AMAT, MU
CPU Box Makers:	GTW, HWP, IBM, DELL, SUNW
Technology:	CSCO, MSFT, ORCL, XLNX
Retail:	WMT, HD, WAG, LOW, GPS
Telecom:	T, GTE, NXTL, PCS, QCOM, FON, WCOM

To reduce risk, adjust share size based on the sectors' volatility.

As you have learned in previous rules, certain sectors, for whatever reason, tend to be much more volatile than others. For example, Internet stocks tend to be more volatile than most other technology stocks, which generally tend to be more volatile than pharmaceutical stocks, which tend to be more volatile than oil stocks. This can be concluded simply by looking at charts of the various sectors and noticing the differences in both up and down movement throughout the course of time. The greater the extent of movement either up or down, the more volatile the sector is. As you become more experienced at trading, you will be able to quickly recognize the more volatile sectors.

Once you have identified the volatility of various sectors, it is important to have a plan for the number of shares that you intend to trade when trading each sector. This number is based on your personal financial situation and your tolerance for risk. We prefer to trade 500 shares at a time of virtually every sector except Internet stocks. Due to the extreme volatility of Internet stocks, we typically will only trade 100 to 200 shares at a time. We have found that most Internet stocks can swing several points in either direction within a matter of minutes. So, even with 100 shares, we are able to make a nice profit. Likewise, if the stock quickly goes against us, our risk is much more limited by only holding 100 to 200 shares, as opposed to our usual 500 shares.

The number of shares you trade for each sector is different for everyone. What is important to understand is that you do need to have some sort of guidelines for yourself so that you do not put too much capital at risk when trading extremely volatile stocks.

Learn the converse relationships between certain sectors.

As we mentioned earlier, sector trading is one of the best ways to minimize your risk in individual stock trading because you are trading sectors that are showing relative strength. But, what you may not know is that each sector typically has a converse relationship to another sector. Following are some observations we've made over the years regarding sector trading.

Whenever oil stocks are up, the transportation stocks are typically down and vice versa. This is because if the price of oil is up, the profitability of the transportation stocks will proportionately be lower due to the increased cost of fuel. Each time the tech stocks are down, the commodity stocks tend to be up. This is probably because if people are panicking about the high P/E ratios of tech stocks and selling them, they are more likely to put their money into safer stocks.

There are many places you can find a list of sectors, but our favorite place is on the Marketwatch Web site at *www.marketwatch.com*. When you go to the site, click on Market Data, then click on Industry Indexes. This will allow you to view a listing of all the major market indices in addition to their daily, weekly, and monthly performances.

Obviously, there are many sectors in the market that have converse relationships. You should be aware of these relationships when you are trading and record them in your trading log. Sometimes they occur because money is exiting one group and entering another. Money is always being rotated from one group into another. Once you begin to learn the converse relationships between each sector, you will be able to determine which sectors to buy or sell and when. This will result in a higher percentage of profitability and minimized risk for your overall trading. This is just one more thing to throw in your bag of tricks that will give you the edge over the novice trader.

Trade stocks with increasing average daily volume.

One of the most widely overlooked factors of technical analysis by novice traders is the importance of trading stocks that are showing increasing average daily volume. Changes in volume help you to understand the true current strength or weakness of a stock, and can also yield clues as to where the stock is headed next in the short term. Volume tells the true story of the stock.

In chart 10 on page 120, you see an example of a stock that is showing increasing daily volume. Notice how the volume bars get higher during the last two weeks. This indicates that more and more people are trading this stock for one reason or another. Next, you will notice that as the volume increases, so does the price of the stock. This is a telltale sign that the stock is going to keep going higher in the short term. Why? Because most likely a large part of the volume increases you see are the result of institutional buying. That's a key that you probably want to be long this stock.

Other than the fact that the stock is likely to go higher in this instance, what else can we learn from this chart? One thing we learn is that the stock is *truly* strong because the price has risen on higher-than-average volume, as opposed to a rise on average volume. Sometimes, a stock will trend higher on average daily volume. While this is not necessarily bad, having average volume does not show you whether or not there are new buyers coming into the stock or whether it is merely rising in price due to some possible manipulation with the stock.

In chart 11 on page 121, notice that the average daily volume is increasing, but the actual price of the stock is decreasing. This is the opposite of the first example, where the stock price was increasing as the volume was increasing. In this case, there are more and more sellers who are getting rid of their stock, as opposed to more and more buyers coming in. This is also a clue that some institutions may be selling their positions. In this case, you either want to short the stock or not trade it at all.

The selling on higher-than-average volume shows you that for some reason there are genuinely a lot of people that are selling their stock. This is different than a stock that is drifting lower on light volume. Light volume selling would merely indicate some profit taking. If a stock is drifting lower on light volume, it is generally not a good idea to short it because it would only take one influx of buyers to reverse the direction of the stock. But a high volume sell-off usually means something is wrong with the stock, and it

Chart 10: Increasing price and increasing volume

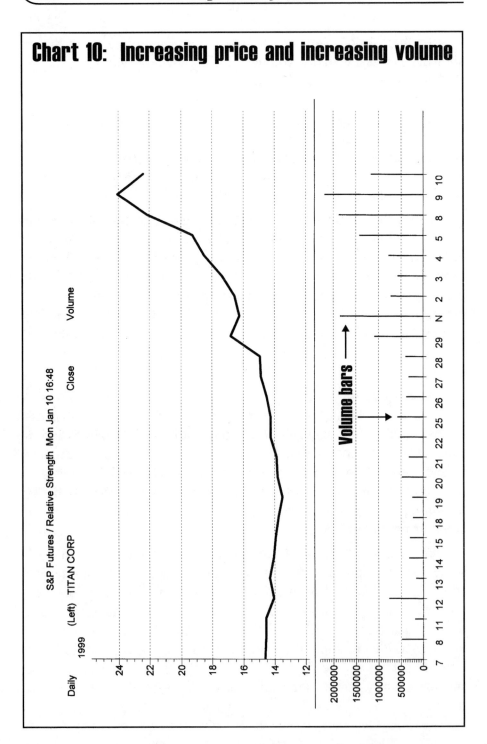

Chart 11: Increasing volume and decreasing price

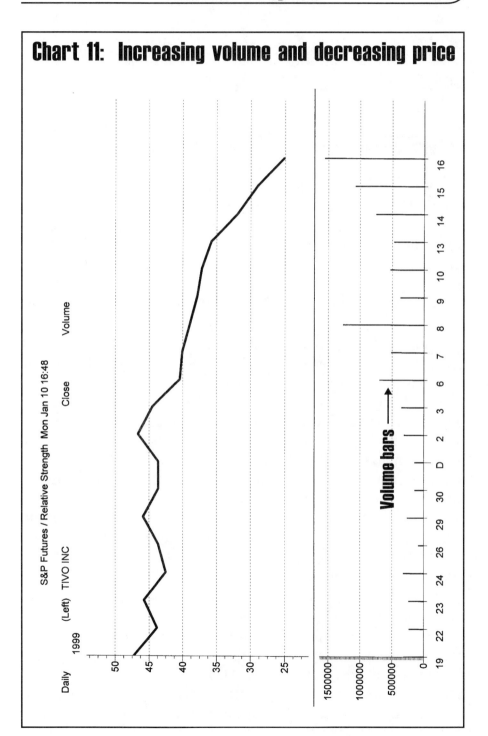

will typically continue to weaken as long as the selling volume remains high. Once again, remember to always trade the leaders of each sector that are showing high average volume, and not the laggards.

Sell into strength, buy into weakness.

When we were novice traders, we always seemed to be trading at exactly the wrong times. Whenever we should have been selling, we were buying. When we should have been buying, we were selling. We knew that our timing was off because many of our trading friends were trading the exact same stocks and making nice profits. But we always seemed to be either breaking even or losing money. This indicated to us that we weren't necessarily trading the wrong stocks, but that we were trading them at the wrong time.

Although getting your market timing to a precise level takes years of experience, there are a couple of general rules to follow that will help you to get your timing right. The first thing to get in the habit of doing is selling into rallies. Many traders fall into the habit of buying as stocks are rallying when they should be selling instead. The problem with buying into rallies is that because you never know exactly when a rally in a particular stock is going to end, you risk the stock's turning around and dropping on you once you buy it. This is also called chasing stocks. Whenever you chase a stock, you typically end up buying the stock at the absolute highest price of the day, and it only goes lower from that point on. If that happens, then you end up panicking and chasing the price of the stock back down in an effort to get filled on your sell order.

The more efficient and profitable way to exit a position is to sell into strength, not buy into strength. One major benefit to selling into strength is that you will be able to easily get out of the stock at the price you desire, and sometimes at an even better price. We have found that our order fills are typically executed at a price that is even better than our limit price because people are tripping over each other to buy the stock. As those people are racing to place their buy orders, we are racing to place our sell order and sell to them. The people that are chasing stocks and buying into rallies are typically the same ones that end up buying right at the high of the day. If you traded the stock properly, you should already be in the stock before it starts running. Then, you will be selling the stock for a nice profit once it starts running. The smart trader is usually in the stock before everyone else figures it out.

One thing that will frequently happen to you whenever you sell into rallies is that the stock will continue to go even higher once you sell it. This is to be expected because it is nearly impossible to determine the exact point at which a stock will top out. But don't worry about it. As long as you are making a profit, it really doesn't matter. Don't beat yourself up because you sell the stock and then it runs another 4 points. The exact opposite could have happened just as easily. Remember that you will never go broke making a profit. Just take the profit and be happy.

Just as it is important not to buy into rallies, you also don't want to be selling short into sell-offs. If a stock is strong and showing relative strength, but has merely dropped down on some profit taking, then you want to consider using that pullback to actually buy the stock, not sell it. By doing so, you will be getting a better entry price that will give you a higher profit once the stock starts to rally again.

As a general rule, you want to be doing the opposite of what the majority of traders are doing. If most people are buying, you should be selling, and vice versa. Although it sounds a bit odd, you want to have the mindset of a contrarian. Doing so will result in lower risk and higher profits.

Buy below the whole number, sell above it.

One of the more interesting occurrences we have noticed when trading stocks is how often the specialists and market makers tend to use the nearest whole number as a frequent resistance or support level for a stock's price.

For example, say a stock in an uptrend is trading at 73 3/4. We have found that the stock will usually trade up to $74 (or just over $74), but will pull back to the 73 3/4 level again before making its next move up past the $74 price. Also, the opposite is true when stocks are selling off. If a stock is at 36 3/16, it will usually drop down to the nearest whole number (36), but will then bounce back up to 36 3/16 before dropping below $36.

This phenomenon is strange because in theory it really doesn't matter whether a stock is bought at $74 or 74 1/8, but we have found that stocks will usually act strangely as they approach a whole number. This is probably due to the fact that, psychologically, investors tend to use the whole number as a price to sell or buy at simply because it is clean cut. Since we know these things, we can put this knowledge about whole numbers to our benefit.

The easiest thing to do is to always try to buy just below the whole number and sell short just above the whole number. Although not following this rule will not be detrimental to you, we have found that you will consistently make a higher profit if you have a little bit of patience by waiting for the right time to buy and sell based on whole numbers.

Another little trick we have learned about whole numbers is to use them to calculate your exact exit point in order to have the highest chance of getting filled on your order. For example, if we are long a stock that is trading at 47 5/8 and we want to sell it, we will typically set our sell limit at around 47 15/16. By doing so, we are more likely to get our order filled because we are trying to sell just below the whole number, which the stock will likely trade up to. Our odds of getting our sell filled at 47 15/16 are much greater than our odds of getting filled at 48 3/16. The exact opposite applies if we are trying to cover one of our shorts. If a stock is at 85 1/4, and we want to cover our position, we will typically place our buy limit at just over the whole number, say, 85 1/8, as opposed to below the whole number, say, 84 7/8. We are more likely to get our order filled that way.

Don't bottom-fish for stocks.

Bottom-fishing means buying a stock specifically because it is sitting much lower than a former high price and expecting it to bounce higher because you bought it at a low price. Let's look at an example of bottom fishing.

Suppose that an imaginary company, BadBoy.com (BAD), traded at a high price of $89 more than a year ago. Since then, it has had negative earnings reports and lots of other bad news. The stock is now trading at its all-time low price of $13 per share. Thinking, "it can't go any lower," you buy the stock at $13 for no other reason than the fact that you think it won't go any lower and is at a nice discount now. This is bottom-fishing.

How do you know when you are bottom-fishing? The easiest way to recognize bottom-fishing is if you look at a stock's chart. If the stock has been steadily coming down during the past several days, weeks, or months, you are bottom-fishing because you are buying that stock based purely on the fact that it is at a low price.

The problem with bottom-fishing is that no one knows where the bottom is. Stocks that are beaten down may never come back. Take Zenith, for example. Many investors hoped that its HDTV technology would bring it back to life. Because of its poor financial structure and high debt, they were forced into bankruptcy. Remember that stocks are cheap for a reason. Instead of buying, everyone is selling.

Likewise, remember that expensive stocks are that way for a reason: Everyone is buying and few people are selling. This is why some of the best investment stocks are also among the most expensive ones. A good analogy to help explain the concept is the example of trying to catch a falling knife. If a knife has fallen off a counter top, catching it by the handle can be done, but it is quite risky. The safer strategy is to let the knife fall to the ground and avoid contact with it. Don't be fooled into thinking a stock will go up simply because you bought it at a very low price. It can, and often will, go much lower. Remembering this simple bit of advice will save you a lot of money.

There is one exception in which bottom-fishing is a good idea, however. This is when the stock is exhibiting relative strength. If the market is tanking and the stock is either staying flat or moving up, then bottom-fishing would be a good idea. Just make sure the stock is showing relative strength on higher-than-average volume. If it shows relative strength to the market or sector, the stock will likely go much higher when the market turns around and runs.

Be disciplined!

If you have been involved in stock trading for any length of time, you have undoubtedly heard many people talk about the importance of discipline. In fact, many of the best professional traders out there will tell you that using discipline is crucial to your success as a trader. We couldn't agree more. In fact, discipline is the number one factor that determines your success as a trader. Let's look at some examples of this.

You buy a stock at $25, hoping for a 3-point gain. The stock rallies to $28. Instead of taking your profit, you get greedy and hold on to the stock longer. It unexpectedly turns around and drops below $25. So, instead of achieving your goal, you take a loss. This is an example of poor money management. You simply didn't have the discipline to stick with your daily profit goal, and you let greed get the best of you. Having the discipline to sell when the profit is on the table would have prevented this situation from happening.

Another example: The market is having a down day and BadBoy.com just announced some negative news, you decide to go short on BAD. You wait for the proper bounce, short the stock, and wait for it to drop back down. However, due to some great economic news that was just released by the Federal Reserve Board, a strong rally in the market quickly ensues, causing significant buying pressure in the stock, which eventually causes it to move upward. Once momentum catches the stock, it flies upward at a rapid pace. Ten minutes later, you are staring at a 2-point loss. Feeling somewhat paralyzed, you still do nothing. Another five minutes pass and the stock is now against you by 5 points. Starting to get a sick feeling in your stomach? Once again, discipline is the key to preventing this heartache. Discipline means you would have sold the stock at a 1/2-point loss, but now you are looking at a 5-point loss! By the way, this is a really easy way to blow up your trading account. Do not let this happen to you. Make up your mind to have discipline, including using your stop losses, and stick to it.

Discipline not only means having the ability to cut your losses and take your profit, but it also means having the discipline to stick to the rules. These rules will become the foundation of your trading strategy and will set you up for profitability. However, these rules only work if you stick to them. Sticking to your rules sounds simple enough, but it is surprising how many people just do not have the discipline it takes to do it.

Realize you are never smarter than the market.

What exactly do we mean when we say that you are never smarter than the market? After all, you have all this experience and education, right? Yes, but the market does not care. Remember that the market is dynamic, and what works today may not work tomorrow. There is never a guarantee that a trade will be profitable, no matter how well you analyzed everything before you made it. The best we can do is to put the law of averages on our side and try to profit by statistically proven methods. But you must realize that there will always be exceptions to every rule.

Whenever you try to fight the market and think that you are smarter, you will lose. It's that simple. When the market changes, and it will, just be perceptive and change with it. You will perish if you try to fight it.

Always consult a chart before entering a trade.

When we first began our trading careers, we were very easily excited when our friends or the media talked about stocks that were moving. We immediately wanted to go out and buy every stock they talked about. We would hear things like, "IBM is going to be a great stock to be in during the next month," or, "You don't want to miss the runup that is going to happen with Yahoo!," we would immediately rush to our computer, look at the price of the stock, and buy it. We realize this sounds a bit simple minded, but that's what we would do. The excitement of others talking about stocks caused us to stop thinking logically.

Occasionally, this type of crazy trading will be profitable, but the goal here is to minimize risk while maximizing gains. Although there are gains to be made if you are lucky, the risk is too high. In our opinion, trading a stock merely because someone told you about it is the same as gambling. Remember, we don't want to gamble, we want to use statistically proven methods that are profitable.

At the very least, it is crucial to always consult a basic daily chart on any stock you consider trading. This helps ensure that the technicals of a stock look strong before you enter a position. It also reduces your risk because you are no longer trading the stock based purely on someone's advice. Typically, if we just want a quick analysis of a stock we are considering trading, we will consult a 90-day daily chart that shows price, 13-day moving average, 50-day moving average, and volume. By looking at the moving averages and volume changes, we are able to determine the strength or weakness of a stock. As you gain more experience in analyzing charts, you will feel much more comfortable entering a position that someone recommends to you.

In the early days of our trading careers, we would look at a chart for the stock after we bought it or sold short. Then, after realizing we made a trade that was probably not in our best interests, we would have to get back out of the stock, only to end up losing our commissions, and often our capital. If we had only consulted a chart before we bought the stock, we would have been less inclined to enter many of the positions that we did. So don't fly by the seat of your pants. Always, at the very least, consult and analyze a chart before you enter a new position.

Have a positive mental attitude (PMA).

When we talk with people about our success as traders, they often comment how positive we are. Some of our friends even joke that we must be on something to be so positive and upbeat. We are happy to report, however, that we are simply victims of something we call positive mental attitude, or PMA.

Positive mental attitude is something we learned about early in our careers, years before we ever placed a stock trade. The importance of PMA stuck with us throughout our various jobs and remains with us now that we are traders. We are confident that PMA is largely responsible for our success.

The funny thing about PMA is that people will often say, "Sure, it's easy to be happy and have a positive mental attitude when you are having so much success in trading." In other words, most people think that we are positive and happy because we are successful. However, it is just the opposite. We are successful largely because we have positive mental attitudes.

Having a PMA is essential to being a successful trader for several reasons. First, it allows you to focus on making profitable trades, even when you are in the middle of a losing streak. Having that focus is essential to being able to snap back on track towards profitability. Without the positive attitude, you will find yourself in a vicious downward spiral. In other words, your negativity will cause you to lose focus, which will cause you to make more losing trades, which will cause your attitude to become even worse, and so on. You will crash and burn if you don't have the proper attitude.

Another reason that having a PMA is so important is that it helps you focus on your profit goals without being distracted by losing sessions. A PMA gives you the strength and courage to keep trading in even the most challenging market situations. It is obviously very easy to just give it up when times get tough, but you will never become a successful trader if you do that.

Have confidence in your abilities.

Confidence is just as important as a positive mental attitude because it enables you to push the button when you are ready to do so. If you don't have confidence in your ability to select the proper stocks and make profitable trades, then you also will not have the confidence to place orders as quickly as you should.

We realize that it is somewhat difficult to have self-confidence if you are not yet a profitable trader, but you need to start by convincng yourself that you already are. It will build your confidence if you can emulate profitable traders. As your skills grow, so will your success.

Be a leader, not a follower.

If you have joined an Internet chat room dedicated to short-term trading, you have undoubtedly witnessed the masses of people who simply follow what the room leader does. Although this can actually be profitable if the leader is good and if you are quick on the trigger, it is not a very reliable or consistent way to make a profit.

Whether in a chat room or on the trading floor, there are several problems with being a follower. The first is that the person you are following does not necessarily have your best interests in mind. For example, the trader might be promoting a stock he or she wants to exit from. As a result, you could end up buying into their sells and selling into their buys.

Your goal is to become a leader so that you can learn how to profitably trade on your own, without depending on other traders. If you learn the necessary skills to do so, you will be much more secure in your future trading career.

By being a leader instead of a follower, you will often be able to score on some opportunities that others may not have even noticed, until the stock has already moved. By being in the front of the pack, you remain several steps ahead of those who are waiting for someone else to show them which stocks to trade.

Study the habits of other traders.

There really is no better way to become a successful trader than to simply be around, and study the habits and techniques of, profitable traders. Since most average investors don't have the opportunity to observe successful traders at work, spend the time to read the interviews we conducted with some of the top short-term traders in the business. This should help you become a more profitable trader.

You should also study the habits of traders who are losing money. You can learn a lot by analyzing other traders' mistakes. If you know a trader who is consistently losing money, try to determine why he or she is so unsuccessful. It will help you avoid making the same mistakes.

Use long-term day trading on your mutual funds.

Although the short-term strategies described in this book are primarily designed for trading stocks, you can easily apply the long-term day trading philosophy to your mutual funds. If we told you all the short-term strategies that you can use on your mutual funds, we'd have to write another book. Some of our acquaintances have been remarkably successful mixing long- and short-term strategies on their funds.

Without revealing their well-guarded secrets, we can tell you that our acquaintances generally invest half of their portfolios in stock index funds, contributing as much money into their 401(k) plans as is allowed by law. With the remaining 50 percent of their portfolio, they transfer between various funds, using well-defined short-term trading strategies. It's easy, it makes sense, and most important, it's been profitable. We are not suggesting that you day trade mutual funds. In fact, most mutual fund companies will penalize you for using short-term trading tactics on your funds. There are ways, however, for you to comfortably combine long- and short-term tactics without breaking the fund company's rules. Keep in mind that some mutual fund companies are more open to short-term trading tactics than others.

In summary, if you use your imagination, you will find that long-term day trading strategies can be applied to almost every kind of investment. Who knows what you can achieve if you apply both long- and short-term strategies to real estate, bonds, and stocks. Your only limits are your creativity and ingenuity.

7.74	-.04	+5.0/A	+7.20/E	+40.30/E	900
7.33	+.01	+3.5/B	NS	NS	569
6.33	+.01	-1.0/C	+8.50/E	+34.30/D	1,048
4.74	+.01	+.6/D	+14.70/B	+35.50/A	230
l0.46	-.81	+64.2/B	+124.30/A	+216.70/A	5,163
1.69	+.01	+23.3/E	+56.00/C	NS	508
l7.07	-.10	+117.4/A	+148.90/A	+270.30/A	1,526
l1.64	+.62	+138.7/A	+240.20/A	NS	650
7.85	-.55	+20.6/D	+100.20/C	+254.00/C	7,619
8.74	+.02	-4.2/B	+8.90/C	+29.20/B	280
8.36	+.01	-5.8/D	+5.90/E	+24.70/D	121
8.43	+.02	-4.5/B	+9.50/B	+28.90/B	710
8.33	+.01	-4.9/C	+8.70/E	+23.50/E	88
8.49	+.02	-4.5/B	+7.90/D	+26.30/C	181
l7.30	-.73	+86.0/B	+162.70/B	+330.30/B	18,257
0.63	-.24	-11.0/E	+5.50/E	+80.90/D	318
8.17	+.02	-4.2/B	+8.60/C	+25.10/D	1,305
6.30	+.01	-4.9/C	+8.00/D	+27.80/D	133
4.57	+.48	+197.0/A	+233.80/A	+423.40/A	6,283
8.29	+.01	-4.9/C	+9.60/B	+25.00/D	159
8.36	+.02	-5.3/D	+8.10/E	+24.80/D	148
6.98	-.48	+17.1/B	+83.30/A	NS	682
0.00	+.43	NS	NS	NS	74
7.22	+.02	+2.4/B	+8.30/C	NS	78
8.30	...	-4.7/B	+8.50/C	+26.30/C	1,595
4.01	+.03	-4.6/C	+7.50/D	+25.80/C	236
3.25	...	-4.2/B	+9.20/C	+27.50/D	1,127
0.46	-.03	NS	NS	NS	94
2.15	+.05	-.5/D	+14.00/C	+35.80/C	1,865
2.30	-.20	+1.9/E	+37.70/E	+105.30/D	1,000
9.44	+.52	+75.3/D	+135.90/C	+315.70/B	5,285
.1.70	-.41				
.1.14	-.16				

ds B:

8.15	+.04
8.51	+.02
7.50	-.47
2.41	-.20
0.34	-.02
4.80	-.15
9.22	-.08
7.99	+.01
5.72	+.05
1.07	+.34
9.81	-.03
0.61	+.04
3.17	-.44
2.44	-.27
6.69	-.24
8.61	+.02
5.07	-.19
1.42	...
8.38	-.35
7.42	-.35
7.34	+.01
2.56	-.13
7.95	+.37
6.49	-.46
0.93	-.28
8.37	-1.04
7.53	+3.17
0.22	-.05
7.71	-.03
6.29	...
4.75	+.01
9.83	-.80
1.57	+.01
5.23	-.09
1.23	+.61
5.96	-.53
8.73	+.01
8.35	+.01
8.31	+.02
8.42	+.01
8.48	+.02
1.92	-.70
0.54	-.25
8.15	+.01
8.30	+.02
1.96	+.35
8.28	+.01
8.35	-.02
8.78	+.47
8.95	+.42
7.23	+.02
8.30	...
3.28	+.01
4.03	+.03
0.42	-.04
2.10	+.05
2:22	-.21
8.11	+.48
9.14	-.38
9.69	-.16

ls C:

2.33	-.20	+14.7/B	+38.30/C	NA	133
1.47	-.15	+22.4/B	+51.90/B	NA	128
3.71	-.46	NN	NN	NN	40
1.00	-.28	+4.2/E	NN	NN	32
3.73	-1.05	+41.3/B	NS	NS	183
0.36	-.81	NN	NN	NN	144
7.78	-.55	NN	NN	NN	61

Nova n	35.70	-1.85	+8.4/D	NS	NS	20
OTC n	87.27	-.13	+104.2/A	NS	NS	66
Ursa n	8.48	+.25	-4.9/D	NS	NS	4

Rydex Investor:

Arktos n	3.94	...	-55.9/E	NS	NS	130
Banking n	6.12	-.45	-29.6/E	NS	NS	21
BasicMat n	7.70	+.02	+2.8/E	NS	NS	8
Biotech n	38.00	+6.94	+221.7/A	NS	NS	372
Electinv n	33.79	+.18	+148.1/C	NS	NS	124
Energy	9.47	+.31	+21.9/D	NS	NS	23
EnergySer n	7.37	+.45	+80.9/A	NS	NS	22
FinclSrv n	7.80	-.49	-16.0/E	NS	NS	28
HlthCre n	8.98	+.02	-10.8/E	NS	NS	16
Juno n	9.40	-.19	+10.7/A	+4.30/C	NS	567
Nova n	35.94	-1.85	+8.8/D	+80.10/B	+269.60/A	2,884
OTC n	87.88	-.12	+105.2/A	+344.50/A	+860.20/A	39
PrecMetls n	4.50	-.03	+3.2/C	-48.90/C	-39.50/C	4
Retailing n	11.12	-1.28	-10.9/D	NS	NS	151
Tech n	27.76	-.38	+75.9/E	NS	NS	48
Telecomm n	18.88	-.65	+48.0/C	NS	NS	3
Transport	5.55	+.06	-28.7/E	NS	NS	31
USGvBd n	8.92	+.18	-10.5/E	+11.90/D	+39.00/D	4
Ursa n	8.54	+.26	-4.3/D	-32.90/D	-55.00/D	388

SAFECO Funds:

Balanced n	10.90	-.17	-4.6/E	+15.80/C	NS	16
CalTFr n	11.02	+.04	-9.6/E	+6.50/E	+29.70/B	81
EquityA p	21.68	-.69	-1.1/D	NA	NS	58
EquityB p	21.45	-.69	-1.9/D	+35.30/D	NS	27
Equity n	21.86	-.69	-8/D	+40.20/C	+134.30/C	1,962
GNMA n	8.95	-.02	-8/E	+13.60/D	+34.50/C	38
Growth n	23.80	+.43	+13.8/C	+48.00/A	+148.70/B	732

▶ **Section III** ◀

Interviews with Successful Short-Term Traders

BalancdA n	11.22	-.15	+.2/E	+35.80/C	+96.60/C	49
BndInxA n	9.98	+.05	-5/C	+16.10/B	+38.70/B	85
CAMuniA n	9.84	-.01	-7/A	NS	NS	103
CapApA n	10.24	-.21	+3.0/E	+58.00/D	+160.50/D	58
CoreFxInA n	9.82	+.05	-7/D	+15.80/B	+40.90/A	2,525
CorpDIA	1.97	...	+3.8/A	+16.50/A	+32.40/C	115
EmMktDbt n	8.82	+.03	+33.6/A	NS	NS	353
EmgMkt np	12.78	-.48	+82.9/C	-.40/D	+24.60/E	1,170
EqIncA n	8.34	-.14	-5.5/C	+28.40/B	+100.30/D	51
EqIndxA n	41.75	-1.26	+10.0/A	+71.40/A	+202.80/A	1,930
GNMA A n	9.21	+.01	-4/D	+14.90/D	+37.90/D	84
HiYid n	9.98	+.01	+2.3/C	+18.30/B	+58.90/A	615
IntMuniA	10.51	+.01	-1.6/A	+11.10/A	+28.00/D	707
IntlDGovA n	9.82	+.02	+.4/D	+15.70/B	+36.10/A	114
IntlFixA n	14.11	-.31	+39.5/C	+65.00/D	+100.30/C	2,336
IntlFixA n	10.25	-.05	-6.9/D	+8.00/B	+26.10/D	896
LgCapA n	33.72	-.79	+26.5/D	+119.40/B	NA	3,494
LgCVaIA n	16.30	-.40	-7.5/D	+26.90/C	+116.50/B	2,889
MidCapA n	15.28	...	+11.1/C	+35.50/B	+125.10/B	34
NJ Muni n	9.68	...	-1.9/A	NS	NS	46
NY Muni n	9.60	+.01	-2.2/A	NS	NS	428
PA Muni A n	10.08	+.02	-1.8/A	+11.60/A	+27.90/B	87
S&P500A n	41.65	-1.26	+9.7/B	+70.50/B	NS	869
ShtGovA n	9.88	+.01	+2.7/B	+16.30/A	+34.10/A	100
SmCGroA n	32.83	+.35	+112.8/B	+130.70/C	+282.60/B	1,334
SmCVaIA n	13.19	-.13	-1.7/C	+6.90/D	NA	610
TaxMgdLC	12.47	-.40	+5.5/C	NS	NS	1,123

SG Cowen Funds:

IncGrA p	9.89	...	-3.9/C	+8.10/E	+80.70/C	30
IFxdIncA p	8.92	-.01	-2.5/E	+12.00/C	+31.70/C	4
LgCapVaIA p	9.66	-.08	+7.8/D	NS	NS	7
OpptA p	12.89	+.28	+43.9/A	+8.80/D	+49.70/C	19
Opptl n	13.19	+.28	+44.2/A	+9.80/D	NA	9
SiFE Trust	4.50	-.24	-19.4/E	+5.60/B	+110.00/B	726

SM&R Funds:

Balan T	20.10	-.17	+12.6/A	+37.20/C	+92.40/C	29
EqInc T	23.15	-.36	-6.4/D	+37.20/C	+76.90/E	179
GrowthT	8.34	-.11	+21.7/B	+58.70/C	+138.50/D	214

SSgA Funds:

ActIntl	11.64	-.18	+31.5/D	+32.80/C	NS	106
BdMkt np	9.44	+.04	-6/B	+15.10/A	NS	289
EmgMkt n	13.00	-.42	+70.2/D	+13.90/C	+36.10/C	406
Grincm n	22.99	-.58	+12.7/C	+90.40/A	+220.20/A	390
HiYidBd n	10.28	+.02	+5.3/A	NS	NS	38
IAM Shares	10.20	-.31	NS	NS	NS	64
Intm	9.98	+.01	+.5/A	+14.60/B	+36.20/C	59
IntlGrOpp p	15.13	-.11	+59.8/B	NS	NS	60
LS Bal p	13.59	-.12	+11.5/A	NS	NS	117
LS Gro p	14.57	-.20	+15.9/B	NS	NS	61

Security Funds:

Bond p	6.44	+.03	-2.9/E	+11.
CapPresA p	10.00	...	NS	
Equity	9.79	-.32	+2.7/E	+54
EquityB p	9.26	-.31	+1.6/E	+50.
EqGIA	19.76	+.06	+77.4/A	+110
GrInc	6.05	-.11	-6.9/D	+11.
MuniBd	9.47	+.03	-4.1/B	+9.
Ultra	13.56	+.22	+58.4/D	+134.
ValueA	17.07	+.02	+30.1/A	

Selected Funds:

| AmShs p | 34.37 | -.86 | +14.7/A | +65. |
| SplShs p | 15.22 | -.51 | +14.9/E | +65. |

Seligman Group:

CapFdA t	29.37	+.85	+75.3/B	+123.
CapFdB p	26.46	+.77	+74.0/B	+118.
CapFdD t	26.48	+.77	+74.0/B	+118.
COMuniA	6.77	+.02	-5.6/D	+6.
CmStkA t	13.50	-.37	-3.9/C	+25.
CmStckB p	13.42	-.37	-4.3/C	+25.
CmStckD t	13.43	-.37	-4.3/C	+25.
ComunB t	51.06	-.92	+97.7/D	+182.
ComunB t	48.86	-.86	+96.2/D	+175.
CommunC t	46.83	-.85	NN	
CommunD t	46.82	-.86	+96.3/D	+175.
FLMuniA	7.15	+.02	-5.0/C	+8.
FrontierB t	16.80	-.20	+45.2/E	+38.
FrontierA t	16.11	-.21	+48.4/E	+42.
FrontierD p	16.81	-.20	+45.2/E	+38.
GAMuniA	7.31	+.02	-5.2/D	+8.
GibGroA	14.53	-.43	+44.1/C	+93.
			+43.0/C	+89.
			+47.8/C	+46.
			+6.4/C	+42.
			141.8/C	+226.
			140.2/C	+218.
			+25.8/E	+85.
			+74.5/C	+18.
			+73.2/D	+14.
			+24.8/B	+81.
			+73.4/D	+14.
			+43.2/C	+89.
			+46.4/C	+42.
			140.2/C	+218.
			+24.8/D	+81.
			-5/D	+13.
			+27.8/D	+52.
			-1.2/D	+11.
			NN	
			-1.4/E	+11.
			-5.6/E	
			-4.9/E	+10.

IncomeD t	12.79	-.15	-5.6/E	+7.
IntlB p	21.05	-.25	+26.8/D	+48.
IntlD t	21.04	-.25	+26.8/D	+48.
LCapVaIA	8.44	-.15	-13.3/E	
LCapVID r	8.31	-.15	-13.9/E	
LCapVaIB p	8.31	-.15	-13.9/E	
LAMuniA	7.52	+.02	-4.7/C	+8.
MassMuniA	7.15	+.03	-7.2/E	+7.
MOMuniA	7.56	+.02	-3.8/B	+9.
MiMuniA	7.84	+.03	-3.9/B	+9.
MOMuniA	7.10	+.02	-4.5/B	+7.
MinnMuniA	7.04	+.03	-5.7/D	+5.
NatlMuniA	7.40	+.03	-5.3/C	+9.
NJMuniA	6.63	+.02	-5.8/D	+8.
NYMuniA	7.45	+.03	-5.8/D	+10.
NCMuniA	7.26	+.02	-5.3/D	+9.
OhioMuniA	7.38	+.02	-4.8/C	+8.
ORMuniA	7.19	+.01	-4.8/C	+9.
PAMuniA	7.22	+.02	-5.4/D	+9.
CAMuHA	5.97	+.01	-5.4/D	+6.
CAMuQIA	6.13	+.02	-6.2/E	+7.
SCMuniA	7.33	+.03	-5.6/D	+7.
SCapVaIA p	7.42	-.08	+2.1/D	
SCapVaIB p	7.28	-.07	+1.2/D	
SCapVaID p	7.28	-.07	+1.2/D	
US GvtA p	6.46	+.04	-2.5/D	+12.
US GovtB t	6.47	+.04	-3.2/E	+9.
US GovD p	6.47	+.03	-3.2/E	+9.
SenbancFd p	8.94	+.04	NN	

Sentinel Group:

BalancedA p	17.57	-.16	-2.3/E	+22.
BalancedB t	17.61	-.15	-3.0/E	
BondA p	5.86	+.04	-1.5/C	+12.
ComStk A p	36.43	-.75	-4.4/D	+26.
ComS B t	36.35	-.76	-5.1/E	+23.
GvSecsA p	9.45	+.06	-1.4/C	+14.
GrthIndexA	21.25	-.68	NS	
HiYidA p	9.20	+.02	+3.2/B	
HiYidB t	9.19	+.02	+2.6/C	
MidCpGrA p	23.43	+.72	+67.4/B	+131.
MidCpGrB	22.86	+.70	+65.6/B	
PA TFA p	11.96	+.05	-4.8/C	+7.
SMGvA p	9.47	+.02	+2.6/B	+15.
SmCoA p	5.76	+.06	+33.4/A	+54.
SmCoB t	5.48	+.06	+32.4/A	
TF IncA p	12.43	+.04	-2.4/C	+9.
WorldA p	19.78	-.21	+22.2/E	+47.
WorldB t	19.57	-.21	+21.1/E	
SentryFd n	13.75	-.38	-9.1/D	+11.

Mark Cook

Mark D. Cook has been a trader for 24 years and operates from his family's 1870s farmhouse in East Sparta, Ohio. Mr. Cook developed the Cook Cumulative Tick indicator and gained acclaim by winning the 1992 U.S. Investment Championship with an astounding 563.8 percent return. In addition to his trading activities, he conducts workshops and seminars for traders around the globe, helping them learn how to make the most of their trading.

Michael Sincere: How did you first get involved with day trading?

Mark Cook: I've been trading for 24 years. I started back in the 70s. At that time, I did position trading, which is trading up to six to eight weeks. I was also an options trader. Back when I started, there were only 24 stocks that had put options and there weren't any indexes, so all I did was equity options. I just kept getting shorter and shorter on my time frame.

Sincere: You've been day trading for quite some time then—even before it became so popular.

Cook: That's true. I was always the black sheep of trading, against everybody's ideal of what a trader should be. Everyone thought I was going to blow myself up. I was ostracized any place I went. Day traders were called every name in the book in the early 80s. I think serial killers had a better reputation than day traders did. Now, I do seminars all over the country to teach people how to day trade. I feel like I've come full circle.

Sincere: Would you consider yourself a swing trader?

Cook: No, I'm what you call a scalper. But swing trading is how I learned the business. Most of the trades I made were on a two-week horizon. When I studied my trades, though, I found that the majority of time I would make money in a three-day window. If I went beyond three days, the parameter I was looking for diminished in probability. I found I needed to narrow the time frame. Now my crystal ball gets hazy beyond a week. I only do trades that have a 75-percent probability of succeeding. If I feel by my indicators that there is more than a three out of four chance for success, I will do the trade.

Sincere: How many trades do you make on any given day?

Cook: I probably do 20,000 to 30,000 contracts a year. I do three to 11 round-terms a day and average 17 to 18 trading days a month.

Sincere: That's a lot of trading. Can you give us an idea what your day is like?

Cook: Each day I perform what I call a daily ritual. I decide what the probability is of an up day, a down day, or a sideways day. Then, I gauge which has the highest probability and I trade in that direction. I really analyze and formulate a plan for what I think the environment is and then I trade in that direction. I'm doing the type of trading that people say doesn't work!

Sincere: Are you saying that you consistently make money when statistics say more than 95 percent of day traders don't?

Cook: Yes. In fact, one time I was at a seminar in California and this guy got up on stage and started beating the table saying, "No way can you make money day trading! Absolutely no way!" Finally I yelled out, "I guess I've been living a lie for 15 years! Because my trading account sure has grown!"

Sincere: How consistent has your performance been?

Cook: Over the years I've averaged between 85 to 95 percent winning days. I recently analyzed my performance. For a period of 45 months, I had more than 87 percent winning days. I traded 699 days and made money 601 days out of 699. I average about plus $2,400 dollars per day, which doesn't sound like a lot, except that average also includes figuring in my losing days. Once I had a streak of 82 days in a row without a losing day. Then I had another streak of over 50 winning days in a row. If you get into sync, you can rattle them off. Then all of a sudden, you will be out of sync and you will lose three or four days in a row and wipe out a couple of weeks or maybe a whole month of profits.

Sincere: Why do you think you've been so successful?

Cook: I am a very hard worker. I love the markets and I study them. I've been in the business over two decades. I'm an old-fashioned tape reader. I can tell the underlying pressures of the market, underlying buying and selling, and I make that determination. I call myself a blue-collar trader. I go in every day, I work hard, and get a wage. I'm like a mouse. I take a little piece of cheese and then I run.

Sincere: Were you always so successful?

Cook: No. I lost money every year my first five years of trading. I couldn't understand what I was doing wrong. At one point, I reached a plateau where I made a little bit of money and lost a little bit of money, but was able to stay alive. Finally, after about three years of that, a light bulb went on and the consistent winning started. My motto, which I got from Linda Raschke, is "If you continually trade, you will make money." That's what I believe. If you keep doing trades, you will get in sync with the market.

Sincere: How did you maintain a positive attitude for five years when you were losing?

Cook: I didn't say I did. Somebody took my money and I wanted it back. I am very relentless in that pursuit. I couldn't concede that someone else was smarter than I am, that someone had more guts and determination than I did. That was not going to happen. So I studied and studied. Up to that time in my life, I had always succeeded at anything I tried, so I couldn't understand what was happening to me. I really had some bad situations. If someone had been sponsoring me, they probably would have fired me. But it was my own money and I wasn't going to fire myself and I wasn't going to give up. I knew that if I kept my nose to the grindstone, I would get there.

Sincere: So basically what you're saying is that a day trader needs to be able to deal with losing. Can you teach that?

Cook: That is a good question. You can try. The question is are you prepared to lose before you win? Anyone who has been successful in anything, especially trading, has terrible scars. We all have horror stories. They are in our past and maybe in our future, but we learn how to control those situations and we don't quit.

Sincere: I think many other people would have given up after a five-year losing streak.

Cook: I am the hardest worker whenever I am losing money. I think I am best when I am backed into a corner and weakest when everything is going well. When I am backed into a corner and they are beating on me and I'm sitting on my rear end, I start flailing and I will prevail because I am a terrific fighter. I actually have to back off after I've had a succession of winning days. In fact, my business plan for next year is, if I get 30 consecutive days without a loss I'm going to take a week off. Why? Because when you win, you begin to think you are infallible. I call it "walk-on-wateritis." But the energy level dissipates and you get sloppy.

Sincere: Why do you think so many others fail at day trading?

Cook: Everybody wants to make too much money too fast. The greed factor takes over and greed is not the reason to be a trader. If it is, it consumes you and your rationale is gone. I always tell people, I hope you lose money on your first trade, because anyone can handle winners; few can handle losers. My first five years I lost money even though I had 87 percent winning trades. For a lot of people, day trading is a fad type of mentality. Young traders just starting should take that old rule about the singles hitter to heart. The ones who persevere are not trying to make a killing immediately.

Sincere: What do you mean by being a "singles hitter"?

Cook: In day trading, you need to go for the single hit rather than the home run. You have to stop being greedy and stop looking for the one big trade that's going to make you millions. The $2 stock that goes to $100 is so rare that it is almost like winning the lottery. I have made millions of dollars and I've made it by making just a few thousand dollars a day. But I do it day in and day out. So you need to forget about trying to hit the home runs. You can make a fortune by simply hitting singles.

Sincere: But how do you keep greed from entering into your trading?

Cook: Both my great grandfather and grandfather were farmers. I remember once when I was a kid, I asked my grandmother how they did for the month. She said not too well, they had only made $90 for the whole month. And here I am, I can make $125 bucks on one tick in one minute. My grandmother worked herself to the bone for $90 in a whole month! So I think, why am I not willing to take that? The problem for lots of people is that greed just takes over. They don't stop to think how many people would give their right arm to have access to that amount of money in such a short period of time.

Sincere: What would you say is the most important ingredient for success as a day trader?

Cook: If you had to have one ingredient, I would say you better be a competitor rather than someone who goes along with the crowd. If you are not aggressive, you probably aren't going to make it. When you see someone who is in every competitive thing, they've got the fire, they've got the energy, all you have to do is channel it in the right direction and go from there.

Sincere: How long would you say it takes to become a good trader?

Cook: I have people who come up to me and say they want to make money in six months and I say forget it. If you want to be a doctor, you don't walk in the first day of class and say, "Give me my diploma, I'm going to be a brain surgeon." People don't look at trading that way. With trading, you can make more money than any brain surgeon or any profession outside of being a baseball or football player, perhaps. But you have to pay your dues. I tell people it takes three to five years. It's just like tuition costs and the losses are the tuition. Five years from now you should be in the plus column if you have any type of mental dexterity and if you have that fighting instinct and can persevere. What happens, though, is people are quitters. They have to realize that perseverance is what pays off. It is an endurance race, not just a sprint.

Sincere: Psychology seems to play an important role in trading, doesn't it?

Cook: The more mature and experienced the trader, the more he will tell you that psychology separates the men from the boys and the boys from the wannabes. People have to go through what I call the evolution of trading. You have to come to know your own personality, your limitations, your temptations, and your strengths and weaknesses. The only time I lose money is when I lose sight of the psychology of my trading and get myself into a situation that I know is not going to work and is not suited to me.

Sincere: Could long-term investors use what you have learned and apply it to their own investments?

Cook: I think they could, but it would have to be done gradually over time. I remember being trained in the early 70s. Back then, no one who bought a stock would think about selling for at least 366 days because of the tax implications. They brainwashed you into thinking that you had to hold onto a stock for long periods of time. It's going to be difficult for a long-term investor to switch to day trading. Their minds just don't work that way. They would have to do it gradually.

Sincere: What do you think is the biggest mistake people make when trading?

Cook: I teach seminars in my office and I have a lot of people that come in whom I call bleeders. They have lost money and they're bleeding, and if they don't get the bleeding stopped they're going to die. When these people come in, I look at their trades and see immediately where the problem is. It's always that they have been in some longer trade and just won't admit it's a loser. People have to admit when they are in a losing position. If you can liquidate from those losing positions, you can go into the next trade. You have to convince them in their minds to change their time horizon, but that's the toughest thing to do overall.

Sincere: Do you use special equipment when you're trading?

Cook: I have what you call a dumb terminal. I am totally illiterate when it comes to computers. The dumb terminal is a receiver that has quotes on it and I see them run as a tape. I'm an old-fashioned tape reader. I just watch the prices. I do have software that provides a high-speed feed so I can go back and look at trades in a certain situation. For example, if I am out of the office I can go back and look at what happened in a certain time frame and catch up with my reference work and get attuned to where the market is. But I'm a feeler trader. I've got to see the action and as I see the action unfold, I'm a total contrarian. I go totally against the flow of the majority because I feel the majority is wrong.

Sincere: You go against the crowd?

Cook: Yes. I especially love going against institutions. I think they are the most uninformed.

Sincere: What's the best advice you ever received?

Cook: It's a conglomeration of advice from a lot of people. If a trade doesn't work, face up to it. Step on your ego a little bit and step out of your position. I think ego is the worst enemy of the majority of humans in any endeavor. My dad always told me to work to stay small. Don't try and get too big for your pants size. A lot of traders, probably big ones you've heard about over time, get a lot of press and handle major amounts of money. I don't want to give anyone a hint of an impression that I can handle a hundred million dollars. I know I can't. I don't think anyone can. They distort the market so much they become position holders. If you look at their percentage of return over time, I can do better. If I can't make 50 to 100 percent a year on my trading capital, I'm not doing my job. I don't manage other people's money but I advise a lot of people and floor traders.

Sincere: Which markets do you like the best?

Cook: I make more money in a bear market. From 1973 to 1976 was one of the worst bear markets we had and then the market dried out. The worst market of all I think is the docile or the sideways market.

Things just completely dry out and there's no interest and the volume and volatility drops off. Those are really tough markets. That is every trader's dread. I learned in that environment and because of that I learned how to survive. I look forward to bear markets.

Sincere: So you make money on both the short and long side?

Cook: Just give me a market that moves and I can make money. If it is going up or down, I don't care. Markets always go down faster than they go up and you can make a lot of money when you short. You might be able to double your money in minutes or hours where on the upside it takes a little more time.

Sincere: Is there any time when your trades are more successful than any other time?

Cook: Some of my best times have been around serious news events such as the Persian Gulf War. This was a very good trading time for me. Any situations where there is any type of trouble in the world news builds uncertainty. Uncertainty builds volatility and volatility brings the amateurs into fear mode and that is when I clean up.

Sincere: How about the after-hours market?

Cook: I'm a liquidity king. I do pretty big sizes, so I have to be able to get in and get out. That's what I look at. I don't mean get in and get out at a profit, I mean just get in and get out of a trade. In 1982 I got stuck in a position that became totally illiquid and I couldn't trade out of the mess. I need to be in a liquid market so I can easily exit my position. Right now, after-hours is a little too illiquid for me, but I'm sure that will change at some point.

Sincere: How else do you minimize risk?

Cook: I always put a bid or offer at a certain place. I don't like market orders. A stock has to come to my price, otherwise I don't touch it. I am also very contained. I trade S&P stocks and the bond futures. That's all I know and I don't profess to do anything else. I've tried others, but I always come back to and do very well in those markets. I have a feel for them. I think you have to avoid the areas where you are not gifted, not talented, or not really comfortable. That is a sure recipe for disaster. I keep things very contained and I've learned those markets that I trade very well.

Sincere: How do you know when to take profits?

Cook: One of my rules, the most hard-and-fast rule, is I will not let a profit turn into a loss. If that happens to me, I feel like I'm lower than low. If a trade is moving in my direction, I will scale in and scale out. I might take a profit and still leave money on the table. If it goes higher, I take some more money off and I scale down that way.

Sincere: So you don't use any technical data to help you decide when to sell?

Cook: It's more a feel that I have. If I think I've made enough money and it is a good return in a short period of time and you can put that in your pocket, then I take my profits. There's a fine line between being a greedy person and being a rational person. Am I thinking a stock is going to go higher because I want to make more money or am I thinking that way for a rational reason? Most times, when I look at a trade, I decide that a bird in the hand is worth two in the bush. I'm a very short-term trader. I like to close my office door at night being flat so I can enjoy my family. And boy, you sleep well at night!

Sincere: You seem to rely quite a bit on feelings and intuition.

Cook: Intuition is something that can be acquired, but again, it is not today, tomorrow, next week, next month, or two years from now. Developing intuition is something that takes time. Anyone who is great at whatever they do can feel when things aren't right, but that comes through experience. You have to convince people that they have to spend the time and money to learn and get that experience. If you're willing to put all the ingredients to work, you can have some degree of success. If you don't want to take the time, forget it, you're just kidding yourself. You might as well go out and play roulette.

Sincere: Do you go on margin?

Cook: I actually don't. I am a cash trader. Preservation of capital is essential. I'm not as hungry to make big money because I don't feel I need it. I'm not one of these guys who want to be worth 100 million dollars. I don't aspire to that. I want to be comfortable with what I have. The game now is keeping score against myself. That's all I care about. Trading to me now is fun. I tell people, if something is fun and entertaining you will never work a day in your life. I've been blessed because I can make about as much money as I need. I wait for the right market setup and then I aggressively pursue it. I sense opportunity and abstain from risky traps such as dull markets.

Sincere: A lot of people dream about becoming a day trader. What are some of the benefits of day trading?

Cook: I have some day-trading friends who have the lifestyle they want. They have financial and emotional independence. They can live any place they want; they can work when they want; buy anything they want; and can control the people around them by choosing their friends. These are some abstract benefits of being a day trader. The satisfaction of a job well done is where you can control your own destiny with unlimited earning potential in a stimulating vocation. Trading allows you to achieve what you want out of life.

Sincere: Do you have any advice for would-be day traders?

Cook: You need to make your own decisions, your own interpretations, and try to keep external influences and distractions to a minimum. I'm in a rural area of Ohio and this helps me to trade more effectively. I don't want to get any type of external news clouding my judgment. If I see an article, it might distort my thought processes and possibly push me in one direction or another.

Barry Dorfman

Barry Dorfman is president of Trader's Choice, Inc., which is involved with start-up operations, management, training, and marketing for Wall Street trading firms. Barry is a profitable swing trader who has been day trading for approximately seven years. He also gives private consultations on everything from the basics of trading to advanced techniques.

Michael Sincere: How did you first get involved with day trading?

Barry Dorfman: My brother, who is the vice president of a large day-trading firm, offered me the opportunity to come in and see what day trading was all about. I went in and was both intrigued and fascinated by the hundreds of traders—young and old alike—who were making money on a regular basis and learning how to do short-term trading.

Sincere: When you first started, were you successful right at the beginning?

Dorfman: No, it took me approximately 18 months before I became profitable. Some traders do it in month one; others take three or four years. The whole concept is to keep a trader's losses down to a minimum while he's learning to trade. Once he learns how to trade and it clicks, as we say, he can make back any losses sometimes overnight, and then he can be profitable on a regular basis.

Sincere: Could you explain how a beginning trader would keep losses to a minimum?

Dorfman: You have to accept that you're going to lose for a period of time until you start making money. Very few people make money day one or month on, very few; those are the best of the best. In my firm, they say it takes at least 12 months before a person learns to trade—and that's with hands-on training on a regular basis. Since you know you're going to lose money while you're learning how to trade, you should start out small. Start off with small shares, like baby steps, and do lots and lots of trades and make little mistakes first. Then, move up to 100 shares and make lots of mistakes at 100 shares. I'd rather go home losing $100 at the end of the day than go home losing $1,000. Once you consistently see your profits exceed your losses, you can start what we call stepping up the share size, going from 100 to 300 to 500 to 1,000 shares. When you're trading 1,000 shares, you will be able to make up all those little $100 losses in a very short period of time. In the early stages, accept that you are going to lose. When you start small, at least you won't lose as much, and you'll be able to make the smaller losses back at some point in the future.

Sincere: What was the biggest mistake you made during those 18 months?

Dorfman: I traded too many stocks. I'd be in two tech stocks, two drug stocks, two Bells, two oil stocks—I was all over. I had to find my niche. I had to find the stocks that I felt comfortable with. That took me maybe six months. Then from there, I needed to work on my timing. It took me a long time to learn how to time my entry and exit points. When the market opens up big in the morning you can't buy stocks right away. You have to wait a certain amount of time for the market to stop moving a bit before you get involved in a stock. Timing took a lot of time to learn.

Sincere: Where did you find your niche? Which stocks do you trade?

Dorfman: I do not trade the Internet stocks, so I will typically trade the technology sector because those are in play and there is a range to them. That is, they move, as opposed to trading a stock like GM or Chrysler, which may only move 1/8, 1/4, or 3/8 of a point per day. It is very difficult to make money trading with those types of stocks. I prefer to trade moderately volatile stocks and will typically trade groups that are in play for the day. Today I'm trading tech stocks. If the drugs are in play for the day, I will trade the drug stocks. If the telecommunication stocks are in play, I'll play those.

Sincere: What do you mean when you say a group of stocks is in play?

Dorfman: When a group of stocks is in play it means there is action somewhere. It could be because of earnings, or news, or potential mergers. Once I find there's action, I'm going to trade it. And I'm going to trade stocks that have at least a 1 1/2-to-2-point intra-day range, so I know I'm guaranteed to make something, not just 1/8 of a point, for all my effort.

Sincere: When you say you're trading a group of stocks, does that mean you're trading stocks in the same sector?

Dorfman: Exactly. We call it sector trading. I buy the leaders in the sector or group. If the drug sector were in play, I would trade the leaders in that sector. If you are looking at the drug sector, for example, you might see Bristol Myers-Squibb and Merck up $4, while Johnson & Johnson or Abbott are only up 1/4 of a point. I would call Johnson & Johnson and Abbott the laggards; Bristol Myers and Merck the leaders, so I'm going to invest in them. I won't trade the laggards. At first it may be hard to identify the leaders, but those are the ones you want to be in. Don't think that the laggards are going to catch up to the leaders because it never works that way.

Sincere: What indicators do you look at?

Dorfman: If the Dow is up 50 points and the drug stocks are up 3, 4, or 5 points for the day, and they all have huge volume, at least 100 percent of the five-day volume, that's the sector and those are the stocks I want to be in. That trend will typically last for a couple of days. It's not usually an afternoon quick shot: It's usually a two- or three-day cycle.

Sincere: So you buy several stocks in the same sector?

Dorfman: That's correct. It's also a good strategy to buy all the stocks that make up the sector if you have the capital to do so. At my trading firm, we buy the whole sector. When the market takes off, we are selling into the momentum. Then we wait a bit for the market to calm down and look at which of the stocks in the sector are the strongest. We might get back in with only those strongest stocks with a bigger share size and sell into the momentum again. Individual investors might not have the resources to buy 10 to 15 stocks in a sector, so they would be better off sticking with the leaders.

Sincere: Why do you trade several stocks in the same sector, as opposed to just picking one?

Dorfman: Different stocks in the same sector will move at different time intervals. Typically a lot of stocks will just move based on the fact that the market is moving. As the futures go higher and the

Dow Jones goes higher, the stocks will typically go higher, too, but different stocks will go higher at different times. You really never know. You're putting the odds in your favor by taking several stocks from the group or the whole group. Then when the market starts going up, you'll see which ones move better than the others will, and you can get in and out of those.

Sincere: Which stocks should a novice trader start with?

Dorfman: That's a personal decision. You should try to trade stocks that have a lot of liquidity, a lot of volume. Know where the institutions and money-management people are. When you decide which stocks, which group you want to invest in, you put them up on your screen so you can visually see them on a regular basis with your indicators in one area. Then it's just a matter of trading in and out and watching where you develop a personal affinity for a certain group. I found that I was able to get a feel for trading in and out of the drug stocks and the technology stocks. I didn't feel the same way trading the Bell or the Dow stocks. The average investor at home could buy two or three stocks and look to make 1/4 point after commissions, but that's not very practical and not effective. It's also not easy. It's much easier to identify a sector that's in an uptrend and buy one or two of the leaders and trade them during the day or for a couple of days while they're in play.

Sincere: That's relative strength?

Dorfman: Yes, it's relative strength trading. It is finding where the action is, where the strong stocks are, which are the stocks that are moving and hopefully will be strong and have momentum for the next several days. When you trade these types of stocks, you can generally stay in that position for two or three days without getting hurt.

Sincere: How important would you say shorting is to a short-term trader?

Dorfman: I think that everybody should learn to short. The better longer-term traders that I know of have made more of their money on the short side of the market than the long side even though we've been in a bull market. Stocks will come down faster than they go up and there are bigger down sides than there are up sides. Every stock has a cooling-off period where it dips down and some of the volume comes out. This will allow you on the short side of the market to make some money.

Sincere: What do you call your style of trading?

Dorfman: I'm a momentum swing trader. As I said, I'll buy six, seven, eight, 10 of the strongest stocks as a group and tie them in at the same time. As the market takes off in whatever direction I'm looking for, I sell into that rally. When other people are buying, I'm selling to the people who are buying. I can do this because I am in a position long before it makes its move, not while it's making a move. I'm selling to you when you're buying it—and I'm selling it to you at a higher price.

Sincere: Do you have a daily or weekly profit goal?

Dorfman: At our firm, we teach you to set a profit goal of a certain number of points a day. You can set your parameters wherever you want, whether it's $500 or $1000 a day. Let's say you set profit parameters for a trade at 5 points. The idea is to sell when you make your 5 points. If it goes up 5 more points, no big deal. Or, if you have 5 points in the stock sell half your position and hold half of it. So now if it goes up 5 more points, at least you'll be in the game for another 5 points. If it goes down 5 points, you're still not giving back all the money you made, so you would have been positive on the trade. It's a very good idea to take some profits off the table. When you make your goal, leave. If you're making 1 point a day and you're trading 1,000 shares, that's $1,000 per day. Anybody will tell you that's very good living.

Sincere: Is that what you do?

Dorfman: Actually, yes. I add up all my 1/4s, 1/2s, 3/4s or whatever I've netted, and, if I've made my profit goal, I'm done by 10:30 or 11 a.m. Then I might go home, relax, and come back at 2 p.m. You reevaluate the market at 2 as if it's a whole new trading day. What was strong in the morning will not necessarily be strong in the afternoon, so you reassess the whole market for half an hour and then you start trading in the afternoon.

Sincere: Do you have a preference between the NYSE and NASDAQ stocks?

Dorfman: Eighty percent of my training was in the New York stocks. I like NYSE stocks because if I want to buy 10,000 share of IBM I can put an order in and get it filled at 10,000 shares of IBM at the price it was at. To buy stocks like Microsoft on the NASDAQ where you have to play with the market makers and get partial fills makes it much more difficult. Now, however, the larger NASDAQ stocks, like Microsoft, Intel, or Cisco are much easier to trade and have a lot more volatility and range, so I prefer trading them. I like stocks with a minimum volume of about 5 million shares per day, so there is liquidity.

Sincere: How long did it take you to develop your trading style?

Dorfman: It takes time. I think style is directly related to your personality. Everybody needs a foundation to start trading. You need to know the basics of trading, stock selection, how to time in and out, the basics of discipline and risk management. That's what I concentrated on first. Then, you have to consider your own personality. Some people like to trade Internet stocks with lots of volatility and huge up and down swings. Others prefer to trade the small blue chip stocks and take small fluctuations and small price swings. You have to let your personality decide which stocks you want to be in, and develop your trading style based upon what fits.

Sincere: Could an online trader at home do what you're doing on the Internet?

Dorfman: Absolutely. I think that if you can narrow down your stock selection to 20 stocks and trade the leaders in those groups, you can very easily make money in any market on a regular basis. You want to put the percentages in your favor by trading solid stocks that have good liquidity, where the fund managers and institutions are playing. They are not going to be manipulating the prices. You cannot manipulate Microsoft and Intel, for example. Either of these stocks is going to stay strong for a couple days. Just because somebody sells a half million dollars of Microsoft doesn't mean the stock is going to plummet 10 points. You can safely watch and follow these stocks at home. Go with the leaders, go where the action is, but trade less shares. As you build up your equity, you can trade more and more of these larger stocks effectively and make money.

Sincere: What equipment does a new day trader need to get started at home? Is Level II really necessary?

Dorfman: You would definitely need to have data feeds so you can get quotes. You would also need an order entry system so you can make your trades. I think you can do quite well with Level I. In fact, from my point of view, Level II is more confusing than it is helpful.

Sincere: Some traders claim that holding an overnight position is very risky. How would you respond?

Dorfman: Holding a position overnight can be risky in certain situations. You need to be aware of numbers such as consumer confidence, unemployment numbers, and any news or earning announcements on the stocks that you're holding. For example, if I know that Merck is making an earnings announcement in three days, I would prefer being out of the stock before the earnings come out. If you're taking a stock into earnings, that's gambling in my opinion. So holding a position overnight is risky if you are taking positions into numbers or into earnings. If it's a normal day and you know there's nothing significant, like Greenspan is not talking about an interest rate hike, you can usually be safe in taking the stocks overnight for a few days.

Sincere: How about margin? Do you believe individuals who are just getting into trading should go on margin?

Dorfman: Trading on margin can be detrimental to a novice trader because it allows him to trade more stocks and more shares than he's capable of handling. A 2-1 margin is the highest I would advise. In my experience, I've seen people lose more money given 10-1, 12-1 margins. Instead of trading 100 shares of Yahoo! and Lycos and Amazon, they use margin to trade 1,000 or 2,000 shares. When a stock sells off 20 points or all three of them sell off 20 points cumulatively, you're down $20,000 instead of only $1,000 to $2,000. Most traders can't take that kind of a loss. You really shouldn't be trading more money than you have or you will have to stop trading and won't have a chance to make it back. Money management is crucial when it comes to trading.

Sincere: What do you mean by money management?

Dorfman: Money management means learning how to keep your losses small and take your profits. Lets say you started with a $50,000 investment and now you're at $100,000. You may want to take some of your $50,000 out. You should always protect your money, always keep in mind that the next trade you do could be sloppy or a really bad losing trade. Remember that the market can turn against you and you can lose your money. When gamblers are playing blackjack, they instinctively know when to take some of their chips off the table. When the tables are getting cold, they walk away. I walk away from trading all the time. You have to know your parameters. If you feel uncomfortable in a day trade or you cannot find a stock to trade, then you shouldn't be trading.

Sincere: Is poor money management the reason so many people lose money?

Dorfman: People lose money for a variety of reasons. A lack of knowledge or education or perhaps they trade rumor stocks or stocks they hear about from friends. But the basic problem is that people get too greedy. When some people make a profit, the greed kicks in and they want to do it again and again, so they keep trading. Before they know it, it's noontime and they're in the hole. They're going to lose more money trading between 12 and 1. Now it's 2 and they're going to be trading crazy and take positions home with them overnight. This is what happens. It's all part of the discipline. For most people, when they hear that the guy next to them or the guy down the block made 10 points that day, they say, "Oh, I've got to stay here in front of the screen and make more." What's going to happen is you're going to keep on giving back profits, trading more, turning more commissions, which are going to eat into your profits. You have to be disciplined and follow the rules you set for yourself.

Sincere: Even though you may know the rules, you still need to have enough discipline to follow them?

Dorfman: Absolutely. You must have discipline. Without discipline, you're going to lose money. By far, discipline is the hardest thing to teach. Timing in and out of the market is difficult, but that comes with time and experience. But discipline is extremely difficult. People just don't want to be wrong. They're not willing to check their ego at the door and come in as a humble person. The market will beat you up because the market is stronger than you are. If you have some bad days or some bad weeks and you're trying to make all this money back and force your trading, that's the worst. You have to be able to be emotionless. It is very, very crucial to develop those discipline skills while you're trading 100 to 200 shares of stock, not when you're trading 1,000 shares.

Sincere: Do you think it's important for traders to maintain a daily log?

Dorfman: Definitely, it is very important. Each day you need to have some type of a trading log where you can talk about your mistakes, the things you should have done better, why you got into a position, why you got out of a position, what's in play, what to look at the next morning.

Sincere: What information do you keep in your trading log?

Dorfman: If you're trading as a profession, you need to pay attention to the market and the activity of the universe of stocks you trade. You need to look at where your stocks closed relative to the market, where the market closed relative to itself, which stocks in the group were the strongest, which stocks were the weakest. You need to study your own performance and see what you did wrong and what you could have done better. You need to spend at least an hour after the market closes to review your universe of stocks and you need to spend at least an hour before the market opens to review your notes from the night before. By doing this, you can get a feel for where the market is opening up, how stocks behaved the day before, what trend you're in. Then you need to develop a game plan, that is, a strategy for approaching the market that day.

Sincere: Why is the log so important?

Dorfman: If you don't document each day and learn from your trading, you're not going to see patterns in the stocks or in your performance. People will always remember the one winning trade, but they never seem to remember the small losing trades. You need to review what you've done right or wrong and make a change in your trading. You also need to have an exit position for every trade you put on. You have to know that point in advance, not figure it out while it's happening. And you need it there in front of you, to visually see it, to remind you. You just need to be prepared. I have little index cards I put up on my monitor to remind me of what I need to work on. It might be "take your profits," "let your stocks run," "the trend is your friend." I look at these cards every day before I start to trade as reminders of whatever I need to work on for that particular week. I have a strategy, I have a game plan, the market opens up, and I'm there! If you do not have a game plan for the day, you should not be trading, because you're just gambling.

Sincere: Can you give us an example of how you might use this information to help you decide what to trade?

Dorfman: Let's say you see Intel, Microsoft, or Cisco up 5 points every day for the past three days. You decide to get in on the fourth day. The stock goes down 4 or 5 points right after you buy it. Why did that happen? You weren't watching what was happening in the market. If you were watching, you would have noticed that it was showing signs of what we call relative weakness. Even though it was up big for three days, when the market ran up, the stock did not go up. It was showing signs of weakness. What I might do the next morning is short that stock instead. When you study your logs, you'll be able to get this type of information and use it to become more profitable.

Sincere: Is there one rule you never break?

Dorfman: I never take losers home with me. That's the number one rule for me. If I have a stock and at 3:59 it is against me, I will never hold the stock until the next morning, hoping that it will bail me out. I will sell it and take my losses.

Sincere: Even if you bought it as a swing trade?

Dorfman: No, that's different. I'm talking as a day trader. I've learned over the course of my training to avoid taking losing positions home with me hoping they'll bail me out the next day. We have found that generally, these stocks will continue to go down in the morning.

Sincere: But on a swing trade, would you let it go a little further?

Dorfman: Absolutely. With day trades you have to have very tight stop losses. With swing trades you can let yourself go a little bit more. You really need to be more focused in on the fundamentals and technical analysis in swing trades. However, even if you're taking it for a swing trade, what happens if you're down seven points with big volume? Do you really want to take that home with you? I would be reluctant to take something home like that. Maybe it's normal in a swing trade when you're holding a position for a few days to have 1/2 point, 1 point, or even 2 points against you. But when a stock sells off hard on the close and you don't have the staying power or the money in your account to hold onto it, then you can see yourself wiped out.

Sincere: Do you ever average down or up on losing positions?

Dorfman: As a rule, I don't. I won't say I've never done it, but only under some rare circumstances. I remember there were some shots fired overseas in the Middle East in 1995 and the news came across CNBC intermittently throughout the day. The news had nothing to do with the stocks, but the market just tanked in response to the news. I couldn't get out of my positions, so I averaged down and bought low. When the news dissipated and everybody breathed a sigh of relief, the markets flew back up to where they were and I sold my positions for a profit. So, if something comes up that's beyond your control and you think it really has nothing to do with the stock you're in, there's no reason why you shouldn't average down.

Sincere: But as a rule, would you say it's not a good idea for a novice trader?

Dorfman: As a rule, if you're in a stock and the stock is not acting well, get out of it and look for something else to trade. Cut your losses. When I'm wrong, I know I'm wrong and I get out. That's the reason the best traders know when they're wrong and can reverse themselves on a dime. Most people would probably rather lose millions than admit they were wrong. If you are wrong, get out of your position and look for something else. Not get out of your position and sit there and cry, but get out of your position, analyze what you need to do, and get back into something else.

Sincere: Would you say that cutting losses is the number one rule for a novice trader?

Dorfman: And learning how to control your emotions. Most traders just panic in a losing situation. The emotions paralyze them. A smart trader, with no emotion, gets in and out of his position and looks to find where he was wrong. The sign of a professional trader is you get beat up and you come back. A novice will sit there and just keep on taking losses. He will sulk and cry, he's embarrassed to go home and tell his wife about it, and he's embarrassed to tell his friends about it. The next day, he's trying to make back that money with vengeance trading. Vengeance trading is by far the worst trading to do. When you lost money in a particular stock and you keep on going after that stock, it's going to get the best of you. You're going to lose more and more, so its best to just get out of your loss like a man or woman and look for the next trade. The loss is done. You might not make it all back at once, but you can make it back slowly.

Sincere: I can see where traders might lose confidence when they start losing. How can they break the cycle?

Dorfman: The key is to bring your confidence level back up. Everybody is going to go into a down period. Even the best of the traders will experience periods of time where their trading is not going to be good. It's inevitable. But you've got to learn to deal with that psychologically. You can't be saying to yourself, "Oh, I'm losing, I'm the worst, I'm terrible." You've got to be positive. You go back over your risk-management techniques and your rules and try to decide what it is you're doing wrong.

Sincere: What should you do after you figure out what you're doing wrong?

Dorfman: Instead of looking to hit home runs, you look to hit singles and doubles for the next couple of weeks and slowly make back your money. Try not to go home any one day with a negative. If you made $100, go home with $100. The next day go home with $200; the next day go home with $50; the next day go home with $300; the next day go home with nothing, flat. All those little singles will add up and you'll start saying, "Wow, I made back a portion of my money and I'm getting my confidence back."

Sincere: Any last words of advice for the novice short-term trader?

Dorfman: Never take a winning day and turn it into a losing day. That is by far the most defeating thing psychologically for a trader. That's why I say take your profits off the table. You want to leave a little bit of profit on the position so that you can run, swing trade, or go short, but always take some profit off the table as soon as you can.

David Nassar

D avid S. Nassar is president and CEO of Market Wise Securities, Inc., an online broker-dealer, and president and founder of Market Wise Stock Trading School, L.L.C. The Market Wise School has taught more than a thousand people from around the world how to trade electronically, using state-of-the-art technologies and strategies. Many of these trading strategies and techniques were illustrated in Nassar's best-selling book, *How to Get Started in Electronic Day Trading* (McGraw-Hill). He is currently at work on two additional books and also conducts regular seminars to educate the public on electronic trading techniques.

Michael Sincere: How did you first get involved with day trading?

David Nassar: I didn't start out with day trading. My introduction to financial markets began with my father. He spent 47 years in the financial services business and would come home and teach us about IRAs when they first came out, and mutual funds and all the new investment products that were coming to the market. I started investing in stocks when I was a junior in high school through an investment club, and by college was trading actively. I was actually a classical chartist and charted my own stocks on graph paper.

Sincere: Did you ever consider yourself an investor?

Nassar: To me I was investing because I would hold my positions for periods of days and weeks at a time. I took my profits very early, even from the beginning, and started making money pretty quickly. It wasn't until I thought I knew all the answers that I began to see losses.

Sincere: Is there a secret to lasting in the business?

Nassar: I think there is a secret: Be humble. As I said, I went through a stage when I got cocky and I thought I had all the answers. It was then when I gave back more money than ever. So I learned the more humble you are, the more you respect the market. A little fear is good for you in the market.

Sincere: People don't seem to have that right now.

Nassar: You're right, I don't think the fear factor is there for the average investor or online investor. They think it's easy because it's a raging bull market. They think, "I'll trade something and if it doesn't go up right away, I'll just give it a few weeks and it will come back." I think the people that really understand fear are the day traders.

Sincere: Why do you say that?

Nassar: As day traders, we don't give our trades time to develop to the upside or downside. It either happens quickly or we're out, one way or the other. Even though we haven't had a true bear market for a while, I think we actually, as day traders, feel the effects of a bear market every day or every so many days.

Sincere: Can you give us an example?

Nassar: Yesterday was a good example of a bear market on a one-day basis. I think it's important to understand my mindset yesterday. I don't mind telling you I lost $13,000 because I went long on a stock that I shouldn't have, and ended up giving back $13,000 just like that, just because I was fighting the trend. The point I'm trying to make is that active traders who engage the market every day that don't hold long-term positions, really do know how to trade in bear markets. We see the market from that one-day perspective.

Sincere: So when a real correction or a bear market comes, the day traders may come up better.

Nassar: I absolutely believe they will. There's no doubt in my mind.

Sincere: Because it's the long-term investors who think they're holding forever.

Nassar: Right. When something goes against a longer-term oriented investor, their paradigm is to hang onto it and it will come back. So that gets back to your original question, do I think that the average investor has fear of the markets? The answer is yes, to a degree, but not at the level of fear and respect they need to have.

Sincere: I noticed from one of your seminars that you actually break day trading down into different strategies. Could you explain what a day trader is to you?

Nassar: To me, the definition of a day trader is a couple things. On the more mechanical side, a day trader is a person that has true direct access to the market on a level playing field with tools like Level II, ECNs, SOES, Select Net, and Super Dot. That's a very small, small percentage of the makeup of a day trader. From a more technical perspective, a day trader's point of view should be multidimensional, whether it's an intra-day, intra-hour, or multiple-day trading discipline. Whether someone makes a bunch of trades every hour, every day, or every few days, these all could be considered day traders. I don't think he who trades the most wins. Quite frankly, he who profits the most wins, and there are plenty of people out there who could profit very strongly just by making a few trades a day or a few trades a week.

Sincere: Would you call yourself a swing trader?

Nassar: I would call myself a multidimensional trader. Most of the time, I always have positions working over a series of days like I do right now. Right now I'm long about 3,000 shares of stock in the technology sector, which I'm holding because of some technical patterns that I see in the stock that might take as long as five to 10 days to develop. I'm also invested in mutual funds so I don't trade all of my money, and I never have. I have always been diversified that way. This is a multidimensional approach and is what I endorse. I am, however, careful not to enter a position as a day trader and change midstream into a swing trader.

Sincere: Do you think intra-day day trading is the most difficult strategy?

Nassar: I do think it is the most difficult. With the cost of software, commissions, and taxes, you've got to be more than just breaking even in your trading to make a profit. When I make a day trade, I'm always looking for a bigger point movement than just a teenie or 1/8. I'll accept a teenie or 1/8 if I don't like the way the stock is acting. If I can exit the trade with 1/16 or 1/8 profit, I'm not exiting for the profit, I'm exiting because I don't like the way the stock is acting. Obviously, my motivation for getting into the trade in the first place is for a larger point movement than that. I'm looking for 1/2-point moves or even multiple-point moves depending on how volatile the stock is.

Sincere: How do you make the decision to trade a particular stock?

Nassar: It's instinct supported by data. It's data that's fed through your head through Level II, how stocks are printing, how the stock is testing at key levels, whether it's the close from the previous day or a new high. My favorite technique by far is looking at how active a stock trades at each price level. You can get to know stocks so well. Say a stock goes from $85 to $87. When the stock trades hard and heavy from 85 1/2 to 86 1/2, that tells me a lot more about how it will trade from 86 1/2 to the $87, a segment of that 2-point move. I watch the momentum and try to determine where it is strong and where it is weak. So, I know that the stock is strong from 85 1/2 to 86 1/2, that 1-point range. If it blew right through that to the up-side, I know there's a lot more support in that 1-point move or that 2-point move than if it grinded up slowly for the last 1/2 point. I know the stock will give back a lot more in that last 1/2-point move than it will in that middle-point move.

Sincere: So you look very closely at price levels?

Nassar: I use thick or thin to describe how a stock trades at each price level. If a stock burns through price levels quickly, it's thin because there's not a lot of liquidity. For example, say a stock is going to trade from $85 to $86. If it burns from $85 through all the fractals— 85 1/8, 1/4, 3/8, 1/2, etc.—right to the next price level or the next handle from $85 to $86, then it's not very liquid at each price level. Conversely, Microsoft is an example of a thick stock. Incredible amounts of volume have to occur at every price level for that stock to move. For example, you have to see 25,000 shares trade at 1/16, another 25,000 at 1/8, and another 25,000 at 3/16, and so on. It is very thick at each price level. If a stock is burning through those levels quickly, that tells you a lot more about the strength of those bids than it does if it burns through very slowly.

Sincere: So would it be correct to say that you are looking at volume?

Nassar: Yes, volume is the jet fuel that makes the whole thing fly. Volume is a representation of liquidity. It shows how many trades are really going off. Let's just say you have 10,000 shares for sale at 15 1/8 and buyers rush in through high volume and absorb all the shares. The faster the trades go off, the faster the stock burns through each price level. The demand exceeds the supply, so the prices go higher. On the other side of that coin, now you get 10,000 shares at 15 1/8 for sale and buyers come very, very slowly to the game, if at all. Now you're saying, "Yesterday I sold 10,000 shares of stock at 15 1/8, but today, I try to sell the same stock at the same price and buyers are barely coming to my doorstep." Volume is lower. As a seller, you're wondering if you should lower your price to get rid of inventory. You want to know the strength of those bids coming into the market, that is, what is the strength of the buyers. That's measured through volume.

Sincere: Some traders say price is the only factor they look at. What's your opinion?

Nassar: I really doubt that anyone could look at price alone and be a good trader. Let me give you my favorite theory in the market. The stock market is all about cause and effect. The cause, which causes prices to move, is the imbalance of supply and demand. The effect is the associated price change that you see as the result of that imbalance of supply and demand. Traders who react to price change are already behind the trade. Traders who recognize the imbalance of supply and demand by reading volume and how quick stocks trade at each price level recognize where the imbalance is by the strength of the bids, or the strength of the offers. If the bids outweigh the offers, or the bulls outweigh the bears, the stock's going higher. If the offers outweigh the bids by the strength of those offers, that is, there are more sellers than buyers, then the stock's going down. If you react to the imbalance of supply and demand you'll be in front of the wave of liquidity and you'll be on the side of the professional traders, not the amateurs.

Sincere: Would you agree that the key to all this is the Level II screen?

Nassar: There's no doubt that the Level II screen is one of the most important tools I use. But all on its own, you couldn't singularly say it's the best tool. It's a great tool with the aid of other tools, like the tape. Without a tape, a Level II screen is a virtually useless tool. Together with the tape, it's synergistic, that is, the sum of the two tools is greater than the individual tools. If you said I could only have two things to use, I'd say give me the tape first and then give me a Level II screen. I would also like charts, but charts are yesterday's news. Charts have already happened, so if I had to give up one of the three in this example, charts would have to go.

Sincere: Even the intra-day charts?

Nassar: Absolutely. The intra-day charts are only a line or bar representation or candlestick representation of what has already traded.

Sincere: What do Level II screens tell you?

Nassar: Level II shows you the size of each trade and the speed with which shares are being traded in real time. The volume tells you the strength of those bids or offers and tells you more than anything else does in the market.

Sincere: Can you give us an example?

Nassar: Here's an analogy that might help. If a building is burning out of control, metaphorically the people in the building are the sellers and they're rushing for the door. The speed at which they rush for the door helps you measure their fear and panic. If sellers are rushing to the market with panic in their eyes, you know that as far as your stock's concerned, it's burning out of control to the downside. On the other hand, maybe the building is just smoking a little. The alarm goes off, but you don't see any real flames, and people walk calmly for the door. Sellers are walking calmly out of their stocks, but it's not with panic and fear. When you look at how fast a stock trades and the size of those trades compared to how fast people are running for the exits of a burning building, you get a better indication of when a turning point might be coming and when to get in or get out.

Sincere: It sounds like what you're saying is that the market is about understanding the psychology of other people.

Nassar: Exactly. The market is about human beings and human behavior and psychology. Stock prices don't move because a company develops a new drug. Stocks move because the company that developed the new drug was able to put a perception in people's mind that caused an emotional reaction. That is why the stock moves. You could cure cancer tomorrow, but if no one knows about it or the perception's not there, people won't buy the stock. Conversely, you could take bull and put a perception in people's mind that it's going to change the way business is done in that industry and the stock will fly through the roof. It's all in the perception.

Sincere: What's the best advice you ever got about trading?

Nassar: This certainly isn't a unique answer, but I think the best piece of advice anyone's ever given me is to cut my losses. It's easy to say and everybody says it, but until you've lived it and you've had your head taken off, it's really tough to learn it. It's one of the most valuable lessons you can learn.

Sincere: Speaking of losses, where do you cut yours?

Nassar: If you try to take a literal interpretation of the market and say you cut your losses at 8 percent, or 2 percent, or 1/2 percent, you're just not going to make it because the market's just not that literal. My losses are cut based on the way the stocks react, based on the momentum, the strength in those bids and offers I told you about, or the sentiment. For each stock, the situation is going to be different.

Sincere: But don't you have some general limits at which you cut your losses?

Nassar: I have some literal levels. I know, for example, that I'm not going to let myself lose $10,000 on a day trade. If I get to the point where I need some literal mental stop to get me out of a trade, though, I've already blown it. I should have gotten out when I recognized the imbalance of supply and demand. To be more specific, let's say you looked at a Level II screen and market makers are joining the offer and the prints are showing that they're coming off at the bid price. This means the sellers are hitting the buyers' bids. Then you see professionals are joining the offer and adding more stock for sale. That's a pretty good indication that the stock is getting ready to turn to the down side. Why do you have to wait until the prices change with it and take your money? Cut your losses right away. You were wrong.

Sincere: Besides being careful to cut your losses, what other ways do you minimize risk?

Nassar: I always have a very good idea when I'm getting out before I get in. People seem to think one-dimensionally, that is, just about cutting losses. To me, risk management really starts with which stocks you trade. For example, are you going to trade CMGI, a very thin stock, or are you going to go with a more calm stock like Sun Microsystems? I believe that risk management begins with the type of stock and the sector in which you trade. First, trade a stock that has reasonable volatility but not one that's out of control. (I always tell people don't walk, run, from IPOs because of out-of-control volatility.) Once you get into the trade, the next level of risk management is to maintain that same discipline throughout the trade. If it's a day trade, stay with a day trade. Don't marry it to another type of trade, like a long-term trade. Stay with the discipline that you set for yourself getting in.

Sincere: In other words, know the reason why you bought that stock in the first place.

Nassar: That's right. And know how long you anticipate that trade to be. I know if I'm into a short-term momentum day trade versus a swing trade. I know that for sure before I start a trade. On a swing trade, I'm lightening up on the share volume dramatically. If I'm going into a day trade, I will be heavier on the share volume, but quick to exit. I stay with whatever discipline I start with.

Sincere: Some people say swing trading is too risky because you are holding positions overnight, especially if you're on margin. Would you agree?

Nassar: It's riskier on one side of the equation, but not both sides. Since you can't control exterior market risk, you need to control what you can, mainly volume of your trades and your time horizon.

Sincere: How would you control volume and time?

Nassar: Volume and time are the two risk factors. The more stock you trade, the more risk you take. The more time you're in the market, the more you're exposed to market risk. So you offset each of these factors like a teeter-totter. If you're going to be in the market for a longer period of time how would you offset the risk? You would lower the share volume. If you're going to get out of the market very quickly through a momentum day trade, you've already lowered your risk by not expecting to stay in the market long in that trade. You can offset that reduced risk with more potential in terms of the size or volume of the trade.

Sincere: Do you believe that people should go on margin?

Nassar: I think a 2:1 margin is acceptable for professional traders. It's not the margin that causes the problem as much as it is the risk parameters. Yes, you double down, so to speak. But to me, it's not about the money as much as it is the principles of trading. If a thief steals only a dollar, he's every bit as much a thief as the guy that steals $100. It's just a question of how much money you've been dealing with. Maybe that's a little philosophical, but I don't think margins should change the way you trade. Whether you are trading with a cash account or on margins, it should not be a factor. I do feel that most people should not trade with more than 2-1 margin.

Sincere: On the other end, how do you know when to take profits?

Nassar: The same reason I know when to cut my losses: The stock is no longer acting well and performing in the fashion I anticipated. In other words, the reason I got in is the reason I'm getting out. It's not a matter of profits or losses, it's a matter of watching for a reaction. If there's still strength in the stock and buyers are still coming in, the strength is there and I'm letting my profits run. If I'm in the money on a trade, I adjust to my mental stops on that trending upward line so to speak.

Sincere: Can you give us an example?

Nassar: Let's say the stock is up 1 point in my favor and the stock starts to show some signs of weakness and starts to retrace a little bit. I'll test a level or two below as it comes down to see if we can find a new support level, or what we call a higher high or a higher low. If the stock is hitting a low, but it's a higher low than the previous low, I'm going to let it go because I perceive that I'm finding higher and higher support levels.

Sincere: How about an analogy?

Nassar: It's like doing push-ups. On day one of your workout you can only do 50 push-ups. One week later, you can get up to 100. You're getting stronger and can do more push ups, but you're eventually hitting a weak point. Every day, however, you are hitting a higher weak point. So I'm setting my mental stops at those higher weak points along the way. If the stock retraces back from $85 to 84 1/2 but holds the 84 1/2 level very well, then I won't necessarily cover the trade. I'm willing to risk that 1/2-point retracement to see how well it holds at 84 1/2. Why? Because if it does hold, there's a good chance when it restarts its up trend, it's going to make a new high to 85 1/2 or $86. So I'll give my stock a chance to work.

Sincere: Do you have any advice for the novice short-term trader?

Nassar: Yes, start slow! Start with a longer time horizon and work your way into more active trading. Don't start out making 50 trades a day. Too many emotions come into play when you're making that many trades. In the beginning, make a couple of trades a day and work your way in slowly. Get used to the emotion. Once you get through it and it doesn't seem like you're skydiving out of an airplane for the first time, you'll be more comfortable with the environment of trading. The key is to survive before you thrive. You don't go into trading actively expecting to make money. You go in to survive at first and then, once you get used to the environment, you learn how to make money at it.

Linda Bradford Raschke

L inda Bradford Raschke, a registered commodities trading advisor, is the president of LBR Group, Inc., and director and principal trader for the Watermark Fund, Ltd. She also manages a commercial hedging program in the metals markets. In 1995, Ms. Raschke co-authored the best-selling *Street Smarts—High Probability Short-Term Trading Strategies.* She also conducts seminars and workshops around the country to help traders develop their technical analysis skills. In addition, Linda has been featured in *The New Market Wizards* by Jack Schwager and *Women of the Street* by CNBC market commentator Sue Herrera.

Michael Sincere: How did you first get involved with day trading?

Linda Bradford Raschke: I started out on the floor of the Pacific Coast Stock Exchange, where I traded equity options. Later I traded on the floor of the Philadelphia Coast Stock Exchange. I traded equity options there, too. When you're trading in the pit, which is essentially what I was doing, you buy 1,000 tickets a day. Any floor trader, by definition, is a day trader. A "day trader" is really a misnomer.

Sincere: Why do you say that?

Raschke: I think nowadays the media uses the word day trader to refer specifically to those people who never carry trades home overnight, or the intra-day traders. Most recently the term seems to be used a lot with "upstairs bucket shops," if you will, those little electronic day-trading shops. In reality, though, all professional traders that I know, including large CPAs that manage a billion dollars, day trade. I don't think people recognize the fact that the average holding time per trade for 90 percent of the professionals out there is extremely short. An overwhelming majority of professionals tend to do the majority of their trades on an intra-day basis. If you are a successful professional trader, the odds are that you will be trading on a very short-term time frame.

Sincere: If day trading refers to traders who don't hold positions overnight, what would you call the kind of trading you do?

Raschke: Some of my trades are in the S&Ps that last three minutes, and then I have other trades, maybe in the bonds, which could last two weeks. I've traded a stock and held it for five minutes and held it for three months. I am known primarily as a swing trader, because that's what I do, but it's all semantics, really. I basically just call myself a short-term trader.

Sincere: Do you ever rely on fundamental data?

Raschke: Never. I rely on price only.

Sincere: How about volume?

Raschke: No, I don't look at volume. Patterns can be correlated with price. I don't have time to look at that much information. Volume is important if you're studying daily charts, but I can get a pretty good sense of whether there is volume in a market or not just by the way it is trading. So I never actually look at the volume.

Sincere: Why do you like swing trading?

Raschke: Swing trading is the least risky type of trading you can do because you're not trying to make long-term forecasts or predictions. All you're trying to do is forecast the next most immediate price move. If you're looking at a chart, you will notice there are constantly patterns of waves or zigzags. Swing trading is doing nothing more than trying to forecast the next wave or zigzag. That's it! Now, that is the same whether you are trading on a one-minute chart, a daily chart, or a weekly chart. So you could be swing trading the S&Ps and be doing it on a one-minute chart and the average time of your trade could be three minutes. You could be swing trading equities on weekly time frames and be holding them for three weeks. Swing trading has absolutely nothing to do with the amount of time that you are in a trade. Any trader that studies classical, technical analysis knows that all swing traders are doing is trying to find the next leg on a zigzag of a chart. A five-minute chart is going to look the same as a daily chart...it will look like a bunch of zigzags.

Sincere: Is sounds like it doesn't matter what you're trading. Is that true?

Raschke: It doesn't matter. I'm just trying to play the next leg, whether it's on an hourly chart or a daily chart. It doesn't matter if its corn. Like right now there might be a place in corn to go from $1.95 to $2.05 and that's really, really cheap. Who knows, six months from now it could be at $3 again but I'm just trying to go in for the next little leg, or the next little piece.

Sincere: Are there any areas you stay away from?

Raschke: Not really. I'll trade anything!

Sincere: Why do you think swing trading is less risky than other types of trading?

Raschke: It's the least risky type of trading you can do because you have a very well-defined risk point. You have a very well-defined stop which, speaking in real generalities, is going to be the last swing high or swing low.

Sincere: How many trades do you make a day?

Raschke: I probably trade six to eight times a day and that might be in different markets. Maybe I make three or four S&P trades a day, and maybe I'll make a trade in the bonds, and maybe one in the currencies, and maybe I'll trade a stock. That's probably representative of what I do.

Sincere: What do you think about traders who make hundreds of trades a day?

Raschke: My goal is to be alive and enjoy my life 10 years from now, not to have a fried brain and be totally burned out in three years. It's great if you're 24 years old and have energy to burn. But show me a 50 year old who's doing that. I think the longer people are in the markets, at least the professionals that I know, they'll all tell you their activity levels aren't what they were when they first entered the business. You just learn to be a little bit more discriminating. You come into the day with a certain amount of energy in your battery. When you trade too much, that's when you start to get sloppy. Maybe they'll be up five digits in the morning, but they'll give it all back in the afternoon.

Sincere: Do you do any scalping for 1/16 or 1/8 of a point?

Raschke: No, that's a game that's not going to last. I think you can do that in very active markets. I think if you get into a bear market, all these people are not going to be around. You couldn't have played that game in '92 or '94 and you're not going to be able to play that game I'm sure in the future. We've been in an exceptional environment for the last three years and there's an old saying, "It doesn't take brains to make money in a bull market."

Sincere: So when the bear market comes, or the correction comes, those people will be gone?

Raschke: It doesn't even have to be a bear market. It could just be a change to more of a trading range type of market, or one where there's not so much money pouring into the system, where it dries up a bit. I think we're entering into that cycle right now.

Sincere: Why do you think that?

Raschke: Most of the major commodity entities have turned up. Obviously there's a huge amount of inflation built into the pipeline that is just beginning to manifest itself. It really hasn't yet, but it's going to. Interest rates have been trending higher for a year and a half. There's been a huge expansion in the global money supply over the last three to four years that's just juiced all these stocks and there's no way that can continue. We've been able to get away with a lot of things in the last three to four years. Turn down those spigots a little bit on the money supply and it takes the zip out of a lot of these stocks.

Sincere: If that happens, would you change your trading strategy?

Raschke: No, not at all. I'm not sitting there playing the 1/8s and 1/16s in a quarter game. I'd love to see a nice wild inflationary environment. I'd make a killing because I like trading the cash commodities from the long side.

Sincere: You've been trading a long time. What has made you so successful as a trader?

Raschke: I think I'm very persistent and I put a lot of hours in. I'm also pretty good about keeping emotions out of my trading.

Sincere: Let's take that a little further. What do you think are the characteristics of a successful trader?

Raschke: I think that most successful traders tend to have a fairly high degree of trade activity. We're not stock scalpers, making 300 trades a day, but we make a lot of trades. As opposed to two trades a week, we're making 20 trades a week, that type of thing. A good trader would also be very aware of support and resistance levels and be more price oriented, watching the price as opposed to the indicators. Most of the successful traders I know are also pretty good about having a conceptual road map in their head. And they know how to take a loss. When they go through a draw down period, they're very, very aggressive about making it back up in a very short period of time.

Sincere: How do you go about making up your losses?

Raschke: You just have to get back in there and be very aggressive and not let your emotions get in the way. You may be angry that the market took money away from you and now you want to make it back up. But if you get emotional about it, you won't be able to get back in there and fight because you would be too upset, or upset with yourself for losing in the first place.

Sincere: How long does it usually take you to make up a loss?

Raschke: Let's say I take a $100,000 loss in two days. I could make that up in a week. You have to get back in there and fight and make it right back up. Most of the successful traders that I know come back very, very quickly.

Sincere: So losing actually motivates you to try harder?

Raschke: Yes. You're going to be your own best trader when you're down. You're much more conscientious, you're going to be much pickier about your trades, and you're going to push yourself a little bit more.

If you've just had a nice fat winning streak, you could start to become a little complacent. You're not as motivated or have as much incentive because you have just made a lot of money. In other words, when you go through a loss or a draw down period, you get incredibly motivated to make it back up. It is very empowering when a trader makes back a big loss. Once you've made your money back, you know you can do it again. It's kind of like you've graduated: Now you've got your degree and you're a professional.

Sincere: Are you competing with yourself or with others?

Raschke: Well, with myself. I'm always competing with myself. I'm always competing to see if I can have a better month than the month I had before, or a better year than the year I had before. I have two or three other traders that I'm sort of competitive with, but primarily I'm competitive with my own track record.

Sincere: Do you keep very detailed records?

Raschke: I go through periods where I'll keep incredibly detailed records for two or three years. Then there have been other years where I've been a little bit more lax in my record keeping. I have to say, though, I always do best when I'm more on top of my record keeping.

Sincere: How do you minimize risks?

Raschke: Well there's a couple ways to minimize risks. The first way is to be conscious of the leverage that you're using. Because I probably do about 95 percent of my trading in the futures markets, inherently there's a lot more leverage than equities. I think sometimes people underestimate the trouble they can get themselves into by being over-leveraged. The second way is to stay in the market for a short period of time. The less time that you're in the market, the less exposure you have.

Sincere: But doesn't that mean it's better to get out of a trade within a day?

Raschke: Not necessarily. It might be five minutes. Anything can happen at any time. It's just a general principal that the longer you're in a position in the market, the more exposure you have.

Sincere: Some professionals would say just the opposite. They'd say the longer you're in, the less risk you have. They say go in for three to five years, that's the only way you'll win.

Raschke: Well, those people aren't traders. Perhaps that's the difference between traders and investors. There's a huge, huge difference. I've never heard a professional trader that has been in the business 20 years say that.

Sincere: How much do you rely on charts?

Raschke: I rely on charts now more than I used to. But not during the day when I'm trading. When I'm trading during the day, I'm pretty oriented toward the price. I don't think you can be sitting there flipping through a whole bunch of charts and be able to concentrate on trading. I'm usually watching some type of quote board. I'll be watching anywhere from 50 to 80 different markets. I could be watching the Dows, the transports, oil, bonds, and more. I can watch the price of all this stuff at once. That's how I was brought up. I was on the floor in the 80s and we didn't have software charting programs. All I had was a quote-tron, in fact I used to have a quote-tron out of my house that used to cost me around $1,400 a month, and all it would do is give you the little quotes. You couldn't get a chart. I used to subscribe to a charting service and they'd mail me weekly charts and we'd all sit around and update them by hand every night. I did that for about 10 years. Now I have three separate charting software programs and two separate data feeds so that if one network goes down, I've got a backup.

Sincere: Do you rely on the computer or the Internet for your research or trading information?

Raschke: No, not really. Computers are just there because they can process and format the data that comes in. I find that the Internet still has too much down time for me. I don't think it's stable enough for me yet, so I wouldn't want to have exposure and have it go down on me.

Sincere: Don't you use the computer to make your trades?

Raschke: No, I just call down to the floor.

Sincere: Could you teach someone what you know about trading?

Raschke: Yes, I could probably teach them in a weekend. I could give somebody my basic tools in two hours and say here's the patterns to look for. But there's so much more that really comes into play. There are so many subtleties and nuances in the way price behaves. For example, price behaves differently at different times of the year, such as around the end of a quarter or around holidays or in bull markets or bear markets. There are all kinds of little subtle nuances that a trader is going to learn with experience. You can tell somebody what to look for but they really have to experience it for themselves over and over again before it becomes second nature.

Sincere: The statistics say that 80 percent of people, maybe even higher, lose money at short-term trading. Why do you think they fail when you and others are doing so well?

Raschke: I'd say the percent of failure is probably more like 95 percent. There are a number of reasons. There are egos and emotions. People get stubborn. They don't know how to take a loss. They're afraid to pull a trigger and make a certain trade. They are all psychological issues. You are going to be your own worst enemy.

Sincere: So basically what you're saying is that anyone could learn the systems but it's the emotion that will determine their success or failure?

Raschke: Yes. People that don't know how to control their emotions are not going to make it.

Sincere: Do you have a set of trading rules that you follow?

Raschke: All traders know in their hearts what the rules are. You never want a loss to get too far out of hand. You shouldn't average losing trades. These are some very basic ones. You shouldn't come in today and start trading if you haven't put together a game plan or you're not prepared, or you're tired or under stress or something like that. You shouldn't fight the tape. You certainly don't want to be fighting the tape.

Sincere: Any others?

Raschke: Well, then you come down to little arbitrary things. These might be different for each person. For example, perhaps you notice that the majority of your losing trades tend to come in the last hour of the day. You might develop a rule for yourself like, "Never trade the last hour of the day." What you need to do is study yourself and start to note your own tendencies. I can tell you one rule I should have and that's not to trade on the last day of the quarter. I always seem to lose money on the last day of the quarter.

Sincere: You said it's important to have a game plan.

Raschke: Yes, extremely important. I spend an hour each night putting my game plan together.

Sincere: Can you give me an overview of what your game plan might include?

Raschke: The night before a trading day, I go through each market I trade. Then I decide whether I want to be a buyer on the day or a seller. With some markets, there is nothing going on, so I leave them alone. Conversely, there are some markets I want to participate in. I basically try to decide if I want to be a buyer or a seller that next day and if there's a certain price level that I want to look to buy or sell at.

Sincere: Do you sell short a lot?

Raschke: I probably make about 70 percent of my money on the short side in the financials. In the cash commodities, I probably make about 70 percent of my trades from the long side.

Sincere: It seems that many people don't understand that you can make money on the short side.

Raschke: I wouldn't speak in generalities because we've been in an exceptional upside environment for the last four years. When trading equities, certainly the majority of the opportunity has been on the upside. All you have had to do is pick your spot, buy the hot Internet stock of the month or the day because it's all been to the upside. I have friends who trade 90 percent of their trades from the short side and I have other friends who trade 90 percent of their trades from the long side. I would have to say that you have to find your niche and specialize in just one thing.

Sincere: Is there more risk to the short side?

Raschke: No, I think it's actually easier to define your risk. Once markets start selling off, they tend to go down faster than they go up. I think once a market rolls over and it's selling off, the longs are trapped and never really get a chance to get out. If you make a short trade, it's very easy at least to see where your stops should go. On the long side, you have to give the trade a little bit more room.

Sincere: Do you use mental stops?

Raschke: It really depends on the market and how that market's moving or trading. I'd say about half of the time I have physical stops in and about half the time I don't.

Sincere: What's the best advice you've ever received about trading?

Raschke: The best advice anybody gave me was not to get too big in any one position. In other words, be very mindful of the liquidity. People don't recognize it's always easy to get into a market. But if you're in a market where the liquidity is limited, it's very difficult to get out, especially if you have to get out. That's where I've seen people take some of their biggest losses, by building too big of a position in a fairly illiquid market. You don't want to be too big in a market where the open interest is low or the volumes low.

Sincere: Do you have any particular point at which you take your profit?

Raschke: I just try to stay with it until it burns a hole in my pocket. It depends on why you made the trade in the first place. Some trades or patterns have a very well-defined profit objective. For example, maybe you buy a retracement and you're simply looking for a retest of the high or a low. In that particular case, it's fairly well-defined when to start looking to take a profit. If you're taking a breakout type of trade where the market's breaking out of a certain level or price area, you might stay with that trade as long as possible. What I try to do is always put myself in a win-win situation. At some point I'll try to take half of the profit off the trade to lock it in, and then I'll try to trail a stop on the other half.

Sincere: Do you have any advice for beginning short-term traders?

Raschke: Start off learning how to do one thing well and don't try to look at too many things at once. Have a lot of patience and do your homework every night. Have realistic expectations; recognize that you are gaining experience every day, even if it was a losing day. Take some time to pat yourself on the back for just pulling the trigger in the first place.

Oliver Velez

Oliver Velez is the president and co-founder of Pristine.com, the nation's leading online educational service for self-directed traders. He is also co-editor of *The Pristine Day Trader*, his flagship product. With a highly successful 14-year record in the day-trading industry, Mr. Velez is often asked to share his knowledge about short-term trading tactics. He recently co-authored *Advanced Tools and Tactics for the Master Day Trader* (McGraw-Hill).

Michael Sincere: How did you first get involved with day trading?

Oliver Velez: My first foray into the stock market actually came through my involvement with an investment club I started over 13 years ago. Like everyone else, I started out by looking at the market from a fundamental point of view. Over a period of time, though, I became disenchanted with what I call "the Rip Van Winkle approach" to investing: Buy a stock today and take a nap for several years and hope you have made money when you wake up. I believe that some very major opportunities were lost or not really capitalized on because of this long-term approach. This realization simply caused my investment time frame to drop consistently throughout the years. Eventually, I was dealing with two to five, and sometimes two to ten-day time periods.

Sincere: How did starting off as a traditional long-term investor help you as a day trader?

Velez: It helped me in terms of recognizing how important, or how superior, the technical approach is. I started my professional career as an accountant, which probably helped me look at the market from a technical point of view. As an accountant, things I was told or instructed to do made me lose a certain degree of respect for fundamentals. I also realized that fundamentals become very, very unimportant when dealing with short-term time frames. We all know that even the very best companies can fundamentally experience a short-term period of weakness. The worst of all fundamental companies can also experience a robust rally over a short period of time.

Sincere: Do you think technical analysis can be applied to long-term investing?

Velez: Yes, it certainly can. The technical approach simply measures what really counts. A fundamental piece of information does not move a stock. For example, an earnings report in and of itself has no ability to move a stock. What it does do is set into motion the psychological and emotional elements that serve as the catalyst for the price movement. What moves a stock's price is how individuals react to a specific piece of information. Instead of looking at the thing that causes the action, technical analysis looks at the action itself. It is a more direct way of keeping tabs on or monitoring the price activity.

Sincere: One criticism of technical analysis is that it can only look at the past, but never the future.

Velez: Technical analysis is no different from what a doctor does when monitoring a patient's heart, or what a heart surgeon might do. A heart surgeon can look at the current pattern of a specific heart and isolate a problem based on that pattern. There are specific reliable events that happen over and over and over again, and these pictures or patterns represent psychological shifts in the market. Trading or capitalizing on any market move is nothing more than determining when the balance of power between one group, let's say the sellers, shifts to the buyers. There is a pattern or a picture of that event. Technical analysis simply isolates the pictures or the patterns that represent these psychological changes. Technical analysis monitors the action itself. It is more direct and deals with the real events, not necessarily the anticipated.

Sincere: Do you look at these patterns to determine at what point to either buy or sell a stock?

Velez: Absolutely. We isolate a select number of patterns that specifically represent turning points in the market, or psychological turning points, which are nothing more than a pattern that represents the shift in power between the buyers and sellers.

Sincere: Could you give us an example of how you use technical analysis to determine which stocks to buy?

Velez: Let's say a stock has experienced three to five consecutive days to the down side. We feel the stock has reached a point where it should be close to some type of reaction back to the upside. That is, after a three- to five-consecutive-day move to the down side, we're looking for the stock to demonstrate support and to rally back to the upside. One of our entry methods would be to buy the very next time the stock manages to trade above a prior day's high. So the three- to five-consecutive-day move to the down side has rid the stock of the weak hands. The rationale is that the sellers have done the majority of their selling. The key sign that the buyers have regained control of the market is that the stock is able to take out a prior day's high for the first time in five days.

Sincere: How many stocks, on average, would you say you or a swing trader might follow at any given time?

Velez: I think the number of stocks one watches should be directly related to the person's ability and their proficiency with the markets. I think, of course, as an individual becomes more seasoned, their list of stocks can grow. Individuals who are just beginning should obviously follow a smaller number of stocks. We start everyone off with a 20- to 25-stock universe from which they can choose potential buys and sells. This is small enough to gain a certain intimacy with each stock. As far as holding positions, we encourage individuals to have no more than four positions on at the same time, and that's on the high end.

Sincere: Why do so many day traders lose money, even after they learn technical analysis?

Velez: I think it is the same thing that causes most people to lose in virtually anything, whether it is business, investing, or day trading. I don't think that day trading in and of itself has a monopoly on a very high failure rate.

Sincere: Can you be more specific?

Velez: First and foremost, day trading calls for a great degree of discipline, which of course is another way of saying it calls for a certain degree of self-mastery. Any endeavor that calls for any measure of self-mastery will always have a high failure rate simply because most people do not possess the necessary discipline. Like any other business, another individual component that leads to a high failure rate is lack of a proper amount of capital. Most businesses fail because they are under-capitalized in America. Most day traders fail because they are under-capitalized as well. Certainly, lack of proper tools and lack of proper knowledge are also factors in failure.

Sincere: How do you define self-mastery?

Velez: I'll summarize self-mastery in one statement: Self-mastery, or the sign of self-mastery, is when you know precisely what to do and then actually do it consistently. Knowing what to do is no guarantee that you'll do it. Most people don't lose because they don't have the knowledge; they lose because they don't possess the discipline. Basically, there are two obstacles to getting to the point where you can call yourself proficient in the market. The first obstacle is knowledge. One has to acquire the knowledge. But after that obstacle is overcome, the bigger obstacle is in applying the knowledge.

Sincere: How important is discipline in determining success in the market?

Velez: We've been training traders for the past seven years all over the world, and there is one common denominator among the losers: Lack of discipline. Most of them know why they've lost. Most of them know the errors they are making. They just don't have the discipline or the self-mastery to stop themselves from making them.

Sincere: Many intra-day day traders believe that it's too risky to hold a position overnight, as swing traders do. How would you respond to that?

Velez: I do not subscribe to this notion that one form of market play is any more risky than another form. It is all risky if you don't know what you're doing. If you know how to play the market, holding positions overnight as swing traders do is no more risky than investing. Any method of trading is risky if you do not have an intelligent way of deploying the specific strategy at hand. All market play is nothing more than gambling if one does not have a plan, if one does not have a well thought-out strategy.

Sincere: Are there specific ways you minimize risk?

Velez: Yes, definitely. One way is to simply draw a proverbial line in the sand. We place a great deal of emphasis on deploying stops, whether they are mental or actual. Before you commit your hard-earned capital to the play, you need to decide up front how much you are willing to lose. It is necessary to know the maximum risk you're willing to take, because it keeps the mind very clear.

Sincere: Are you talking about mental stops or do you actually put in a stop loss?

Velez: Most of our stops are mental stops, which obviously calls for an element of discipline. Whether they are actual or mental, we believe very strongly in curtailing one's risk through stops. Another method of minimizing risk is to change one's lot size. If we feel that a specific play is a takeable play, but in a higher risk category, we'll compensate for that added risk by dropping our size. For example, if we typically do 500 share lots, we'll drop it to maybe 200 shares to compensate for a higher risk play.

Sincere: Have you seen cases where traders increase their risk thinking "this is going to be it"?

Velez: Yes. One of the things we also teach individuals is that trades should be made first based on the maximum potential loss, secondarily on the potential profit. Most novice market players erroneously approach the market in reverse. They see the stars before they see the rocks. We say if you're comfortable losing this amount in the event the trade goes wrong, you have the green light to consider what the upside potential is. We have trainees look at the worst-case scenario first. If they accept that worst case, they can go on to the next step and determine the potential upside.

Sincere: How long does it take someone to become a day trader?

Velez: I don't think it's possible to determine whether you have what it takes to be a day trader in just a few weeks. As a matter of fact, knowing anytime within one year is probably not likely either. You have to become seasoned through trading in many different types of market environments. One can erroneously assume that he is a master trader simply because he has been in a runaway bull market for the past four months. Without experience with some of the more treacherous market environments, he would obviously be making an erroneous judgment.

Sincere: Is there one rule that you never break when you're trading?

Velez: One rule that I would never break is to buy a stock that is outside of my known reasons for buying stock. I try to make that a number one rule for all of my students and it is also one of my rules. Let's say we have five indicators or reasons for buying a stock. If I am buying outside of any one of those reasons, I'm gambling.

Sincere: Could you share some of those reasons with us?

Velez: I will tell you what is not a reason. Buying simply because I see a lot of green prints or buying simply because a stock is rising rapidly to the upside are not intelligent reasons to buy. They are emotional and they are closer to the activity called gambling than trading. Those are not reasons to buy for anyone. Let's say one of my reasons might be that if a stock were trading above yesterday's high, I would buy it. If I am buying for any other reason than because it is trading above yesterday's high, I am now buying outside of my reason and therefore, gambling.

Sincere: But if you're seeing all that green on the screen, obviously there is a lot of movement or volume is up. Isn't that a reason to buy?

Velez: No, it could actually mean that it is more of a reason to sell. Once everyone has already committed, who are your future committers? There is this erroneous assumption in the day-trading community that green prints—you buy, red prints—you sell. It is really a ludicrous concept. There are times when it is appropriate to buy and, at that moment, there just happen to be a lot of green prints, but simply basing your buy and sell decisions on the color of prints or the very short-term direction or movement of the stock at the moment is gambling. That is not intelligent trading.

Sincere: I assume you also make money on the short side?

Velez: Of course. The short side is a very lucrative side for most astute traders. What you'll find when you start to speak with some of the really true master traders is that the majority of their profits actually come from the short side, simply because stocks have a tendency to fall a lot faster and harder than they rise.

Sincere: Would you say you need even more discipline when shorting because of the potential for unlimited losses?

Velez: I think the potential for unlimited losses is somewhat of an over-blown concept. A trader is not going to let a stock run all the way to infinity. But yes, if a stock is trading at $70, of course the maximum loss on the long side is $70. But that should not make anyone feel any better, or feel any safer, about going long rather than going short.

Sincere: Are your rules different on going short?

Velez: Yes. Sometimes it's difficult to go short because it requires that the stock trade on an uptick. Often it is very difficult to establish a short position at the appropriate time. This is what makes shorting a lot more difficult. We actually encourage people to think about shorting only after they have gained a certain degree of proficiency on the long side.

Sincere: On the long side again, how do you determine the stop loss? Is there any formula you use?

Velez: Yes, we have a variety of them. The first stop we call the initial line in the sand. That's when you say, "Okay, this is what I am willing to risk on this specific play." For us, this point is typically below the prior day's low on a swing trade. If we are entering on Tuesday, we do not want the stock to fall below Monday's low for the day. Our stops are usually below the low of the prior day, with the entry day being the current day. Once the stock starts to progress, we move into a trailing stop mode and we adjust the initial stop upward. After two complete trading days, we then move our initial stop and trail it under the prior day's low. The stop is always one day behind. On Thursday, the stop is under Wednesday's low. On Friday, the stop is under Thursday's low. On Monday, the stop is under Friday's low. If we're in a swing trade for more than five to seven days and we have not been stopped out on the down side or our objective has not been met, then we might consider exiting the play based on a time stop.

Sincere: Are there techniques you use when a stock you're holding suddenly gaps down in the morning?

Velez: First, we let the stock trade for five minutes without any activity. Once five minutes have passed, we mark the day's low. If the stock breaks the day's low after the first five minutes of trade, we sell one half the position. Then we let the remaining half trade for the next 30 minutes. After 30 minutes of trading we ask, "Where's the day's low now?" Then we draw the line in the sand there. If, after 30 minutes of trading the stock moves to another daily low, we kill the rest. This allows a period for all of the panickers to get out of the stock. The people who throw in the white towel typically do so in the first 30 minutes of trading. Once they're gone, in a lot of cases, the stock buoys to the upside and you can somewhat narrow your loss.

Sincere: When do you take profits on a winning trade?

Velez: Since our approach is a technical one, we have several profit objectives. For example, after every 2-point move, we believe in an incremental sell approach. We feel that the stock is closer to a pullback with each move to the upside. When the top comes you ideally want to be very light with your merchandise, so you start shedding merchandise as the stock rises to the upside. We have an arbitrary

2-point incremental sell approach. We also come up with other objectives based on prior support and resistance on the charts.

Sincere: Do you hold over the weekends?

Velez: We have to feel very strongly about holding a stock over the weekend but, yes, we will. If we initiate a play on Friday knowing it will be held over the weekend, we may compensate for that slight added risk by dropping our share size.

Sincere: One of the criticisms about swing trading is that it's unwise to go on margin.

Velez: Margin is like every other tool. Used properly, it can be a beneficial aid to the trader; used improperly, it can mean death. It is no different from a knife. A knife in the hands of a skilled chef can carve up a beautiful meal but put that knife in the hands of a child and it could become potentially dangerous.

Sincere: A lot of people have gotten into trading the teenies. What's your view on that?

Velez: Trading the teenies is only appropriate for a small group of market players. Individuals have to determine whether or not they have the psychological and emotional wherewithal to play that style of play. We teach a three-pronged approach to the market. We attack the market from a swing-trading perspective, which is a two-to-five-day time frame. Another method we call guerilla trading, which is a one-to-two-day time frame—buy Monday, sell Tuesday; buy Tuesday, sell Wednesday. The third prong is an intra-day approach, which is buy Monday, sell Monday. We feel that the best traders, the master traders, are never one-dimensional traders. They do not lock themselves into any particular style. There are times when swing trading is more appropriate than any other style, and there are times when an intra-day approach is less risky. Traders who lock themselves into one style are limiting their ability to gain additional profits or lower their risk.

Sincere: So, you're disciplined but flexible, depending on the market, because you can never tell what the market is going to do.

Velez: Exactly. During one period you might be playing more day trades than swing trades, and in another period you might be almost predominantly a swing trader.

Sincere: I know you train people using sophisticated equipment. Do people have to have the top-of-the-line equipment to be successful?

Velez: Being a swing trader does not call for the whole enchilada. It certainly can be beneficial, but it isn't necessary. We encourage people to have two accounts: One account for their swing trades and another account for their intra-day and guerilla trades. The swing-trade account can be a very basic online account. The day trading and the guerilla trading call for your higher-end direct-access systems that have all the necessary bells and whistles to give the individual the ability to slip in and out of the markets with greater ease and efficiency.

Sincere: On a more personal note, what is the biggest mistake that you ever made in your trading career?

Velez: The biggest mistake I made was shorting a stock that had risen exponentially over a very short period of time. My mistake was assuming that a stock could not go up substantially higher after a 225-point move in two days.

Sincere: But how did that happen? Did you ignore your own data?

Velez: Oh, absolutely, absolutely. Every mistake is really the ignoring of a discipline; otherwise it isn't a mistake. What I call a mistake is basically doing something that violates my discipline.

Sincere: Do you use fundamental data at all to decide what to buy or sell?

Velez: No. Ultimately, in short-term trading, we are not buying a company; we are buying or selling people.

Sincere: Could you explain that for us?

Velez: Each time you buy, someone is selling that stock to you. Each time you sell, someone is buying that stock from you. Stocks are moved largely by two emotions, fear and greed. These emotions belong to people. Trading profitably, therefore, calls for the ability to find two groups of ill-informed market players. First, those individuals willing to give up their merchandise at a price that you know is too inexpensive, and those willing to buy your merchandise at a price you know to be too expensive. A trader does not trade stocks, he trades people. That is one of the fundamental things we teach every new student.

Sincere: Are the charts going to reveal who they are?

Velez: The accurate interpretation of charts gives the trader the ability to find those groups. For instance, a pattern of three to five consecutive days to the downside already suggests that a great deal of selling has occurred. Anyone that throws in the towel after that period is basically on the late stage of exiting. Those can potentially be the group that is giving up their shares inexpensively. And obviously on the move to the upside, we're looking for another group that is willing to take the merchandise off of our hands at a price that we feel is too expensive.

Sincere: So by knowing that you're really trading people, then you would apply it to the charts?

Velez: Right, absolutely. Remember, when you approach this whole game from the concept that you are trading people and not a stock, you start looking for the right things. You're saying, "Okay, I'm looking for pain, and now I'm looking for when the pain is starting to subside." Meaning, pain has lasted for three, four, five days. Now the pain seems to be subsiding and now I see the first signs of greed coming back into the market. That is potentially my time to strike. It is when greed or fear turns. After a three-to-five-day period of pain driven by fear, fear converts to greed. That is my entry.

Sincere: In a way, you're saying that charts do not lie.

Velez: Charts do not lie, simply because charts can't lie. They are actual facts. Charts represent where people put their money. A CEO can come on CNBC and talk positively about his company while everyone is dumping the stock. The charts would show up every single one of those sales. If someone buys at 20, it will show up on the chart. If someone says they're going to buy and they don't buy, it will show up as well. People can erroneously interpret charts, but the chart, in and of itself, does not lie.

Sincere: Is one time of the day better than another to trade?

Velez: Actually yes. We divide the day into three broad categories. The opening third of the day is from the opening to about 11:15 a.m. Eastern Standard Time (EST); from 11:15 am to 2:15 p.m. EST, we have what we call the mid-day doldrums period or the black hole. It is during this time that many day traders give up any gains they have earned during the first part of the day. This is typically when the market goes soft and becomes somewhat more unpredictable. After 2:15 p.m., activity starts to dramatically perk up again and in many cases it will continue what it began during the first part of the day. The middle part of the day, then, is more of a time to pause. The sweetest parts of the day are the first and the latter parts.

Sincere: What causes these differences?

Velez: I wish my answer was sexier, but the doldrums are created by people going to lunch. You have market makers and specialists turning their stocks over to junior specialists and market makers with no authority. Their instructions are simply to maintain the market. They aren't supposed to generate a lot of activity. The senior market makers or specialists tell them if something dramatic happens, call them on the cellular phone.

Sincere: How about after-hours trading?

Velez: I think ultimately that it's a very good step, a very necessary step. Access to the market is a right for all. The markets belong to the people and there should be no reason why a person who works a nine-to-five job cannot have access to the equity markets. It will definitely affect how people play the market.

Sincere: Do you prefer trading the NYSE or NASDAQ stocks?

Velez: My preference is with NASDAQ because it is totally electronic in nature. I have found, especially over the last year and a half or so, with the NYSE stocks, there has been a widening of spreads. In the NASDAQ, however, there has been a tremendous narrowing of spreads. The NASDAQ has become a lot more efficient, and in the NYSE, the reverse is happening. The NASDAQ is a cleaner way to trade.

Sincere: Is there a particular sector in the market that you prefer to trade?

Velez: In a very general sense the technology sector is where the volatility is. If my nightly analysis finds there is going to be opportunity in another sector, I will go there.

Sincere: When you trade, do you have a daily or weekly profit goal?

Velez: Having a profit goal is a good tool when you are just beginning. However, as a mature market player, you do not want to place self-imposed limits on yourself. There was a time when I could not break a $15,000 day to save my life. I would come to $15,000 and invariably lose my profits, if not more. When I reached that goal, psychologically, I was done. I lost my motivation to go further. So profit objectives are a tool. They are like training wheels. Once the person has moved beyond the training wheels, the dollar amount is not important. In other words, the dollar amount becomes secondary. It becomes making the perfect trade, trade after trade.

Sincere: Are there other goals a trader should strive for?

Velez: A lot of people come into this game thinking that their first goal is to make money. No, your first goal is to lose less. The second goal is to break even. The ultimate goal is to move yourself into consistent profitability. It really is unfortunate that people come into trading on the wrong side of the ledger. We teach people that professional trading is more a result of learning how to lose than picking winners. My daughter can pick out a winner. Winners tend to take care of themselves. But if a person can show me their records and I see small losses over a period of time, I am looking at a professional. It takes skill to lose consistently small.

Sincere: Is there a particular technical indicator you use more than others?

Velez: Our approach is a technical one, but it is entirely based on price and volume. We use indicators to confirm what we have already decided to do based on the price. For example, say I have decided that XYZ stock is a buy over $40, based on price alone. If the stock demonstrates the strength and ability to trade above $40 and if one of my indicators also confirms that were to occur, then I will use the indicator as a confirming mechanism.

Sincere: Do you look at relative strength?

Velez: We are ultimately trying to find stocks that have a great deal of strength. In an indirect way, this is really finding out where the crowd is. Where is the crowd, what are they most interested in, and let me get in there. That is what relative strength is all about from my point of view.

Sincere: Did you ever average down or up on positions you are losing?

Velez: The general answer is no, but like any answer we will have scenarios where it might be appropriate. When intra-day day trading, never. I should be profitable almost instantly, otherwise, I've entered wrong. Time is the enemy of day trading. We concentrate on such refined entry points that if we are not profitable within seconds we should be out of the play.

Sincere: How about with a swing trade?

Velez: A swing trade is different. On a swing trade, I do not necessarily have to be profitable instantaneously. I am looking for profitability in most cases the following day. Day one is my entry point. If the trade is correct, many times I am profitable starting the following day, and the day after that I am more profitable.

Sincere: Do you keep a trading journal or log?

Velez: I have for years. I analyze every mistake I make. I dedicate a page to each mistake, and write down exactly what happened. I try to determine what caused me to act and try to isolate the error to extrapolate a rule for myself. After a month or two I review the errors to see if I've made the same one a number of different times. If I find, for example, six errors that fall in the same category, I know that I have found my deadliest enemy that could take me out of the game that I love. I dedicate the next period of my life to eradicating it from my very existence.

Sincere: Would it be fair to say that someone should do this?

Velez: Absolutely. Something happens when you transfer an experience to paper. You somehow remove yourself in a very constructive way from the error and you can look at it in a detached way with more clarity. There is also something that happens over time. After a period of time, I go back and review my mistakes. When you revisit your errors, you see them a lot clearer because you are now more distant from this painful experience. Keeping a journal is especially crucial for a person who wants to make a profession out of trading. There is no better tool than a journal as far as I'm concerned.

Final Thoughts

Now that you've reached the end of our book, we hope you'll be able to use what we've taught you to create wealth for yourself and your family. Although making money is an important goal, it is not everything. Try not to forget that money is just a means to an end—it allows you the freedom to decide how you want to live your life. In our opinion, your attitude about money is more important than how much of it you have. After all, money comes and goes, but your attitude about money stays with you for the rest of your life. With the right attitude, you will never be at a loss to find opportunities to increase your wealth.

We have acquaintances that barely have enough money to pay their bills. When we explain that investing in the stock market is an extremely profitable way to increase income, they refuse to listen. These friends are convinced that the stock market is a huge Ponzi scheme designed to help the rich get richer. Their negative attitude about our financial systems will doom any chance they might have to become financially independent.

If you believe you can never achieve wealth in your lifetime, then you will be a victim of your own self-fulfilling prophecy. If you aren't sure what steps you should take to change, begin by believing in yourself. It always amazes us how some of the most successful people in the world believe in what they are trying to accomplish and back it up with action. If you want to make money in the stock market, then make it happen. It won't be easy, but it is possible. Try not to let anything get in the way of your financial goals.

Oliver Velez got it right when he said you are not trading stocks, you are trading people. The stock market brings together all kinds of human beings, all with the hope and desire they'll leave with more money than they brought in. If you can cut through the psychological barriers that ruin so many people's portfolios and focus on increasing profits, you really can win this game. Thousands of people with average incomes have proven that it is possible to make huge amounts of money in the market. If you pay attention, work hard, and never stop learning about the stock market, nothing should stop you from making more money than you ever dreamed possible.

Appendix

The following Web sites are specifically geared to the needs of short-term traders. These sites are a combination of our personal favorites and a list of sites pulled from *Online Investor* magazine. For a detailed description of the most highly rated day-trading sites, read *Online Investor's Source Book*.

Chat rooms

▸ www.activetraders.net
▸ www.pristine.com

News

▸ www.bloomberg.com
▸ www.wsj.com
▸ www.news.com
▸ www.cnbc.com
▸ www.yahoo.com

Charting

▶ www.bigcharts.com

Commentary

▶ www.briefing.com
▶ www.marketwatch.com
▶ www.thestreet.com
▶ www.tradehard.com

Portfolio tracking

▶ www.clearstation.com

Quote providers

▶ www.dbc.com
▶ www.pcquote.com
▶ www.esignal.com
▶ www.trackonline.com

Internet brokers

▶ www.datek.com
▶ www.etrade.com
▶ www.schwab.com
▶ www.dlj.com

Remote brokers

▶ www.abwatley.com
▶ www.cybercorp.com
▶ www.mbtrading.com

- ▸ www.executradeonline.com
- ▸ www.executioner.com

Message boards

- ▸ www.ragingbull.com
- ▸ www.siliconinvestor.com

About the Authors

Michael Sincere began trading stocks through the Internet in 1995. As an early online trader, he researched and interviewed some of the top financial experts in the country. He wrote about what he learned in his first book, *101 Investment Lessons from the Wizards of Wall Street*. Michael is also an experienced corporate trainer, currently employed as a regular columnist for Pristine.com, one of the largest firms for self-directed traders. He can be reached by e-mail at *mikesince@earthlink.net*.

◄ ◄ ► ►

Deron Wagner is an independent trading consultant and professional day trader, currently the manager and head trader of the hedge fund, Intra-Day Investment Fund. He can be reached by email at *deronw@mindspring.com*.

Index